The Jour of a short tour to ... 1822 by John May

Together with the story of the John Mays of Richmond and their relationship with the Southey and Coleridge families

Ian Broadway

To my wife Ann and my family without whose love and support this book would not have been written

BOOKCASE

ACKNOWLEDGEMENTS

I would like to thank Philip May. He gave me invaluable information from his family archives and moreover consented to its being published. He also suggested other avenues of research. The Day Book of John May (the elder) is an historical treasure and one of only two authenticated examples I have found of his handwriting. The other was in The Bodleian Library, Oxford.

I am especially grateful to the staff of Victoria University Library in The University of Toronto, in particular Alison Girling, for their efforts on my behalf in researching the Samuel Taylor Coleridge Special Collection, John May letters. My thanks also go to Ann Leeson for her invaluable work in transcribing certain of the letters.

I am very grateful to Penny Hatfield, College Archivist of Eton College who first tracked down young Johnny May's entry for me and then directed me to other valuable source data.

My thanks to Jeff Cowton and Alex Black at The Wordsworth Trust, Dove Cottage, Grasmere, for enabling me to publish source material. I wish to pay tribute to Tim Wiltshire for his marvellous work in restoring and rebinding the Journal.

I am also much indebted to the following individuals and staff who have helped me along the way: Patrick Hickman for showing my wife and I around Hale Park; Rosalind Passmore for sharing information and suggesting other sources and staff at the Bodleian Library Oxford; Hampshire Record Office; Greenwich Heritage Centre; Keswick Museum and Art Gallery; and the Devon, Berkshire and East Riding of Yorkshire Record Offices.

I have made every effort to trace the owners of all copyright material and would be grateful to hear from anyone whom I have failed to contact for permission.

Finally and especially I want to thank my wife, Ann, who acted as my navigator and companion on the journeys of research around the country and at home.

Copyright: Ian Broadway, 2007
First edition, 2007 ISBN 190414722 4
Published by Bookcase
19 Castle Street, Carlisle, CA7 8SY 01228 544560
www.bookscumbria.com
Printed and bound by CPI Antony Rowe, Eastbourne

Contents

Introduction 5
The Portugese Connection 8
Family fortune – British Factory in Lisbon – Earthquake of 1755- the Mays return to England – Old Friars, Richmond Green – Hale Manor - education under Rev G. Coleridge - friendship and correspondence from 1792 – return to Lisbon – ST. Coleridge, the Frickers, Poole and Pantisocracy – 1796, meets Southey in Portugal, – support of humanitarian ventures – godfather to G. Coleridge's son - Southey sails to Lisbon , John marries,Coleridges moved to Greta Hall – 1802, Johnny May's birth.

1802 – 1822 28
May to to be godfather to Southey's daughter – her death and Southey's move to Greta Hall – godfather to Edith May – war in Portugal – G. and S. Coleridge fall out – Isle of Wight – Johnny at Ottery St Mary – The Wick, – Coleridge and Wordsworth fall out - reconciliation at The Wick in 1812 – friendship with J. T.Coleridge – S. T. Coleridge's at The Wick - Stert and May, wine merchants – gold bullion and the loss of a captured Express Packet – Samuel's Opium addiction – Southey dedication - Eton College – the Eton Rebellion – expulsion – rehabilitation and reconciliation with his father – The Green Ottery Copy Book – Laleham – Exeter College, – Southey's invitation to Greta Hall.

The Journal of a Short Tour to the Lakes 78
Brazilian ventures collapse – set off for the Lakes – Johnny's account – Dr Bell – Grasmere school – infatuation with Sara Coleridge

1822 – 1900 92
Bankruptcy – Oxford and Norwich – Curacy – sells The Wick – Bank of England – Hackney – Southey 'in Bristol – Bristol riots – marriage and Holmpton – Hale Manor – Blackheath –Ugborough – font - family scandal at Blackheath – death of both John Mays - the family vault at St Mary's, Hale – family crest

The Tour 126
Introduction – dedication – Ludgate Hill – Warwick – Birmingham – the Soho Manufactory – Mr Boulton – Staffordshire coal – Colebrook dale – visit to Shrewsbury – Wrexham – Chester – the Rows – Eastham Ferry – Liverpool – Manchester – Blackburn – Garstang – Lancaster – Milnthorpe – Sizergh – Kendal – Ambleside, Rydal, Grasmere – 'Thurlmere – Helvellin – Saddleback – Skiddaw – Keswick – Southey, Sara and Mrs Coleridge and Dr Bell.

References 173
Bibliography 177
Index 178

John May with his father, Joseph.

Introduction

The Reverend John May and his father entered my life at an auction sale one hot June day in 2003. I had long been a collector of tours to the Lake District but had never been privileged to handle an original, and as I believe it unknown, hand-written manuscript.

The binding of John May's *The Journal of a Short Tour to the Lakes* was in a sorry state. Its back was broken and the contemporary boards were loose. The contents however were as crisp and clean as the day they were penned almost 200 years earlier. The Journal has a formal title page and was written at a time when Tours to The Lakes were very much in vogue. From the trimmed, as well as the empty pages, it was apparent that it had first been bound from a larger note book.

Closer examination revealed a number of names, some familiar, some not. The Journal as well as having the signature of John May, dated July 27th, 1822, also carried that of a 'Miss Alice May' inverted on the front free end paper. On the final written page John May recorded meeting Mr Southey, his wife and his eldest daughter, Edith. He was also introduced to Mrs Coleridge, her daughter Sara and a Dr Bell.

The literary connections to the Lake Poets, together with the fact that I did not recall seeing this manuscript in print, excited my curiosity and I decided to carry out further research both into the names I had read and also into the life of John May. I considered that the manuscript, being so clean and clear inside should be preserved for posterity.

The volume was re-bound at Winchester, all as original, in half diced calf, the boards clad with Italian, shell paper and the spine bound in diced calf with the headbands hand-sewn. The signed front free end paper was bound inverted, as found. A label and date were hand tooled in gold leaf.

As a retired chartered surveyor and not having an academic background, I then commenced a fascinating journey of discovery. I met and corresponded with many really kind and helpful people. Originally my researches were intended to be for my own benefit only. Along the way I met Steve Mathews who suggested I might consider publication. My researches then became of an entirely different scale. They have led me by reading, written word, e-mail and the internet to America, Canada, Portugal and Brazil. In this country they have led to Richmond upon Thames, Eton, Hackney, Suffolk, Cumbria, Yorkshire, Devon, and Berkshire. I have followed the lives of families living in Georgian times with considerable wealth and influence whose positions and fortunes were then adversely affected by the Peninsular Wars. The story moved on into Victorian times. They were still well-to-do and respected in the local community but they followed a clerical vocation. My first discovery was that there were two John Mays of Richmond on Thames, father and son. Their lives interacted with the poets and writers, Robert Southey, Samuel Taylor Coleridge and William Wordsworth. They were involved with educational matters such as the reforms of Dr Bell, the Eton Rebellion of 1818, The King's School at Ottery St Mary and Dr Arnold's (later head master of Rugby) private educational establishment at Laleham. And there were matters of the heart with Sara Coleridge; all before young 'Johnny's' ordination in 1825. Johnny May is credited with transcribing some of Samuel Taylor Coleridge's work into the Green Ottery Copy Book deposited at Victoria University Library (Toronto), Canada.

The story really begins with John May (the elder), who was born on 2nd January 1775. He became a wealthy merchant. His fortune came from his inheritance and his trading in the British Factory in Portugal. He and his family occupied property in Bedford Square, Tavistock Street, (then off Bedford Square but since demolished) Richmond on Thames, Hale Manor near Fordingbridge, Clifton near Bristol and a 'Tea Caddy' house at Blackheath. He was a lifelong friend and benefactor of Robert Southey and of the Coleridge family. He lost his fortune variously from the French Wars and bad debts and died at his rented house in Blackheath on 26th May, 1856. He had kept up a regular correspondence with his father at home in England until his father's death in 1796. In fact, throughout his life he was an avid correspondent, with his father, with his brother Joseph at Hale and Bramshaw, with his life-long friend Robert Southey, with Southey's second wife Caroline, with his son John, and with George and John Taylor Coleridge and with various others. Taken together his correspondence reveals a loving, caring and possibly over generous, wealthy family man. He had been brought up to take on the family merchant's business in Portugal but had to diversify with the outbreak of war against the French. Amongst other jobs he had to take was as the first agent of the Bank of England in Bristol.

The primary source data for John May (the elder) is mainly in letters written to rather than by him. They are largely from Robert Southey and from the Coleridge family of Ottery. They are housed in various university and public authority collections. Few examples of John May's own hand seem to have survived. In fact, following the death of Southey on 21st March, 1843, John May requested his son, Cuthbert, to return copies of his letters. In August, 1851 Cuthbert wrote to John May that he could not then lay hands on them but that he would return them.

Johnny May, the son, who wrote the Journal, showed all the characteristics of an easily-led spoilt elder son during his adolescence. He had been born into money but was unwilling to take on the responsibilities that went with it. He had every opportunity to make a success of his education. He went to Ottery St Mary under Rev George Coleridge and then to another leading private educational establishment. From there, aged 13, he entered Eton College on 17th September, 1815. His misbehaviour led to his expulsion from Eton. He then went to Laleham under Dr Arnold before proceeding to Exeter College, Oxford. Johnny, as well as having a rebellious streak to his character, also had an eye for the ladies. He fell in love with Sara Coleridge, the daughter of Samuel Taylor Coleridge.

The Journal kept by him during his 'Short Tour to the Lakes' in 1822 almost seems an act of penance to his family. He admits to having hurt his father and says he hopes to make up for his faults before it is too late.

The formal layout of the Journal suggests either that it was intended for publication or more likely that it was written as a formal holiday task set by Dr Arnold. John May, being a bibliophile, probably had his son's Journal bound at a later date.

Johnny started to grow up when he went to Oxford University. His patience was tried during his curacy at Hackney when he felt that he had been forgotten in his quest for a living. It seems that the Bishop of Winchester, knowing of his past behaviour was quite happy to observe him for a while. After marrying in 1834, at the age of 32, Johnny settled into the family life of a country parson enjoying two livings. A series of ten letters written by him in the period from 1819 to 1850, other family letters and a copy of his great-aunt's diary are deposited in Hampshire County Archives. His ordination papers are deposited at Norwich and a further three letters written by him to his father are at the Bodleian Library, University of Oxford. The manuscript of his Tour to the Lakes is in private hands in England and other family papers are known to be in America.

I have divided divided this introduction into four sections :-

Lisbon

1. The Portugese Connection.
2. 1802 - 1822.
3. 'The Journal of a Short Tour to the Lakes.'
4. 1822 - 1900.

The Portuguese Connection

John May, the father of Johnny May who wrote the Journal, was the second son of Joseph (1730-1796) and Mary, (nee Coppendale) (1745-1824). He was born in Portugal and baptised on 6th February, 1775, in the little chapel of the British Factory at Lisbon. He became a merchant, entrepreneur, venture capitalist and financier; enjoyed great wealth and lost it. He owned beautiful houses and lost them and married an adored wife whom he lost to an early death. The love and respect of his family remained with him to his death.

His father, Joseph, had been born at Lumniar in Portugal on 16th February, 1730, to Thomas May, an English merchant, and his wife Margaret. Margaret was the daughter of Arthur Stert, a respectable country gentleman of Membland in Devonshire, who was to become MP for Membland, Plymouth. Thomas and Margaret were married on 9th January, 1724. Thomas May, himself, was born at Stepney in 1684 and was trading from Lisbon in 1708 in partnership with John Pattison.[1]

Joseph was baptised at the British Factory chapel in Lisbon. He was one of six children. His sister Margaret, also born in Lisbon in 1741, remained single and kept a diary of family events. Joseph was sent home to England to be educated first at Modbury close to Ugborough (where his grandson John was later destined to have a living) and then at Westminster School. He left Westminster in 1745. Rather than pursuing a life in one of the learned professions he was sent to Holland by his father to receive a mercantile education. Extracts from contemporary letters display a love and bond between father and son that was shown from generation to generation in this family. On 24th April, 1747, when Joseph returned to England, Thomas wrote to him: "You know in London there does not want seducers & bad examples, but I hope you'll always be on your guard, & behave soberly & moderately, as you have hitherto done, not to give the least disgust to your relations and friends, & a blessing will attend you in all your undertakings, which will be the greatest comfort to your Mama & me." [2]

Joseph entered the counting house of Mr Thompson, a London merchant trading with Portugal. On the eve of his new posting, on 19th April 1748, Thomas again wrote to his son: "You are now setting forward in the world, but you must remember, that all depends on your own conduct in relation to your future happiness, & I hope you will demean yourself so as not to give the least cause of complaints from your Masters, whom you must serve with all diligence and fidelity: and take care, my dear child, that you don't fall into bad company, which may be the ruin of you in this life & hereafter; always remembering that this advice comes from a father, who loves you tenderly, & is as anxious of your welfare as his own, and whose comfort in a great measure depends on your own behaviour."[3]

In 1751 Joseph moved to the counting house of Mr Massien of Caen where he learned to speak French fluently and made lifelong acquaintances. In 1753 he moved to Lisbon entering into partnership with his father, Mr Coppendale and Felix Mouchet.[4] Aunt Margaret recorded in her diary: "My Brother Joseph May went to Portugal for the first time in the year 1753".[5] The firm was called Coppendale, May &

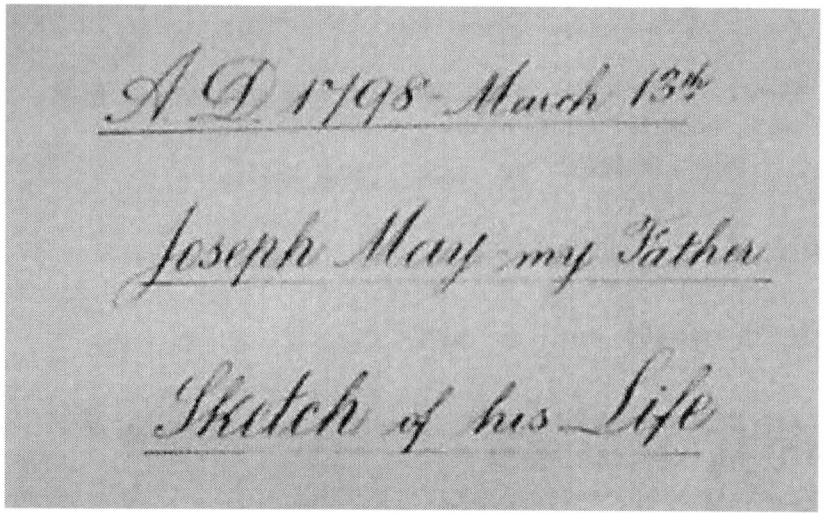

The title-page from John May's Sketch of his father's life in his common-place book.

Co and the Deed was signed by Thomas May 'For my son Joseph May' who may then have been sailing out to Portugal. John Coppendale was allowed £250 per annum to enable him to work in London as well as Lisbon. Joseph was responsible for maintaining the House of Business at Lisbon for which the partnership made him an allowance for "house keeping, bedding, nourishment of Felix Mouchet, of two Clerks and one Apprentice, of a housekeeper, a cook, two footmen and a Porter and servants wages." By 1755 Joseph was a member of the British Factory probably entering under his father's sponsorship.[6]

The families of May, Coppendale, Stert, Livius and Dea were all closely connected. They were all part of the British Factory in Lisbon formed of English merchants and financiers. later their association was reinforced by marriage. Joseph May and John Coppendale continued together in various business partnerships until the Peninsula Wars and political pressures altered their fortunes.

The British Factory in Lisbon was an assembly of merchants and factors. It grew up gradually with enormous privileges enjoyed by British traders in Portugal in return for the political, military and naval assistance given by the British families over several centuries. Many British people were living in Portugal by the eighteenth century. There was a full time Consul and a Chaplain. The Factory had grown up around the waterside of Lisbon where the ships docked. As time went on the wealthier members found houses in the suburban hilly area known as 'Buenos Aires'. Admission to the Factory necessitated being a recognised merchant or factor of British nationality, being of good character and importing merchandise from the British Isles. If the merchant was prepared to pay a Contribution of Funds to the Factory officers he was eligible for membership. Such membership was highly sought after and difficult to obtain.

At the time of the great earthquake of 1st November, 1755, the factory was at its height. Its members were extremely wealthy. A number had returned to Great Britain to enjoy a comfortable retirement. The trading privileges however had been under attack and on 5th November, 1752, the members of the Factory had sent a private letter to the Government regarding duties and tariffs.

Thomas May described the earthquake in graphic detail in his pocket-book for the year 1755:

"Novr. The first of this month God Almighty was pleased to afflict us with two very violent and terrible shocks of an earthquake between 9 & 10 this morning & 1 smaller between 11 & twelve at noon, wh: flung down many Churches, Convents & houses, burying great numbers of the people in the ruins. At the same time there was great agitation & rising of the waters in the river Tagus, by which many persons were drowned & this was succeeded by fires, wh: obliged most of the inhabitants to run to the adjacent hills for their safety, wh: they did in the greatest consternation & confusion imaginable for fear of the fire & rising of the waters, carrying with them relicks & crucifixes in their hands and praying as they went along in great numbers - I then lived in the Chafarir di Analua, and was busy in my garden when on a sudden I heard a most surprising subterraneous rumbling noise, & immediately saw the stone pillars that were near me & supported the Vines rock: The Sparrows (wh: were many) flying about in great confusion, not venturing to settle anywhere, everything being in motion: & two great dogs I had in the garden running up & down the walks very fast & howling in an astonishing manner, & when my family joined me, would not remove from us; in short everything appeared most terrible, the earth moving under our feet like waves and the water that was in a large stone bason (not full) rising & running over its brim. Pray God deliver us from such chastisement in the future. Amen. Amen" [7]

The earthquake destroyed a large quantity of valuable stock and buildings. The May-Coppendale partnership suffered. It was unable to satisfy the claims of its creditors. They, however, with the exception of a Mr Lodge, were prepared to offset some 36%. Lodge insisted on full payment of a bond of £3000, but was prepared to do a private deal writing off only 25%. The other creditors got wind of this and changed their offset to 25% also. The partnership looked for a shortfall of some £18,000. When Joseph visited England in 1756 to attend to his financial affairs, Lodge took measures to arrest him. Joseph had to flee back to Portugal, but at the same time he approached an old school friend, Charles Gore, for a loan of £2000. The loan must have been forthcoming and some time was bought during which other creditors were satisfied. Not so Lodge, however. When Joseph visited England again in 1763 and attempted to settle matters, Lodge refused to do so and again took measures to have him arrested. Joseph once more escaped him by hiding in his lawyer's house for a day and then fled to France by way of Dover.[8]

The Portuguese had lost their possessions and were not able to pay their debts. Indeed they were encouraged in this by their priests, "the major part of whom had absolved them from all their debts preceding the p.mo November."[9] Duties were again an issue and the merchants were anxious to re-establish their business. The members sent a 'Humble Memorial' to Henry Fox, a Principal Secretary of State in April, 1756, ending by asking for "such instructions to the British Envoy & Consul as may be most conducive to the Honour & Interest of the Nation, the Welfare of Trade in general & the Commerce of Portugal in particular."[10] The Memorial was signed by 63 members of the Factory including Arthur Stert and Joseph May. The Government asked Lord Tyrawly to provide a report as he had intimate knowledge of the Factory and many of the papers had been lost. He suggested that the old ways of trading would have to change. They did but the British advantages were being ever eroded. In the spring of 1764 Joseph suffered more heavy loss when a fire burnt down the Custom House at Lisbon. The fire destroyed over one million pounds worth of goods at today's value. As a result, on 31st March, his father Thomas released him from a debt on the condition that he pay 750 millreis annually.[11]

Joseph May and Mary Coppendale, his partner's daughter, were married on 18th July 1764 by the Revd. William Allen, chaplain to the British Factory at Lisbon.[12] This was also the year during which Joseph inherited the entirety of his grandfather's Arthur's Devon estates upon the death of his Aunt, Priscilla Stert.

John Coppendale died in 1764. He had come from a wealthy Yorkshire family with estates at Northoram in the Parish of Halifax and Manor of Wakefield. The estates passed to Thomas Coppendale (Joseph's brother-in-law) who in turn left them to John May (the elder), just at a time when he was experiencing financial difficulty. Joseph May took John Coppendale's widow Rose into partnership on 23rd May, 1764, and, in 1765, she married Thomas Dea, a banker and financier living in Portugal. They returned home to England in June 1772. Thomas died in 1800, and Rose, having been provided for under her husband's will, died in 1806. They were both interred in the May family vault at St Mary's Church, Hale. Rose left her estate divided equally between her son, Thomas, and daughter, Mary May. John May was also to inherit from Thomas Dea's estate. Joseph's father Thomas died in Portugal in 1767, and his widow and daughter, Margaret, returned home to England in 1768.

Thomas Coppendale, the son, was admitted to the Factory on 28th January, 1768, and Richard Stert on August 31st, 1771.[13] On 1st January, 1774, a new partnership was formed between Joseph May, Thomas Coppendale and Pender Luke Stevens. It was known as May, Coppendale & Co. Joseph was planning to leave Portugal and Article 4 of the agreement stated: "That it shall be at the option of Joseph May to reside in Lisbon or in London . . . but as it may be more advantageous for the interest of the House that he should reside in London to transact their affairs he means to go over in the course of the present year for that purpose." He was made an annual allowance for this purpose but was not to charge commissions, brokerage or normal charges. On 4th August, 1775, Joseph and Mary May together with their three children, Joseph, Thomas Charles and John, returned to England.[14]

Robert Southey in his second visit to Portugal provides a description of the situation there in It is contained in a letter written to Lieut. Southey from Lisbon on June 15th.

"Portugal is improving, but very, very, very slowly. The factories have been long declining in opulence; and the Portuguese, who had some years since no merchants of note, have now the most eminent and wealthy in the place. They are beginning to take the profits themselves, which they have suffered us to reap. This is well, and as it should be; but they have found that Cintra is a fine place, and are buying up the houses there as they are vacant, so that they will one day dispossess the English, and this I do not like. Cintra is too good a place for the Portuguese. It is only fit for us Goths - for Germans and English."

The French invasion in 1807 proved almost the final nail in the coffin for the Factory. The Portuguese Court moved to Brazil and it was not until 1811 that the country was really freed from Napoleon's Armies. It was only after Waterloo in 1815 that the French menace ceased completely. In 1810 the British and Portuguese Governments signed a Treaty stopping the setting up of factories in Portugal but adding that this "shall not deprive the Subjects of His Britannic Majesty, residing within the Dominions of Portugal, of the full Enjoyment as Individuals engaged in Commerce, or of any of those Rights and Privileges which they did or might possess as Members of Incorporated Commercial Bodies." The Factory as such ceased to exist but survived to all intents and purposes for another fifteen years. In 1825 the Act 6. Geo. 4., cap.87 repealed earlier Acts allowing the collection of duties on British goods and stated that all funds in hand from the Contribution Fund were to be paid to H. M. Treasurers. The final axe had fallen.[15]

In 1779 a William Gardiner, Esq., of Richmond left the remainder of his estate, which included a property, Old Friars on Richmond Green, Surrey, to 'Joseph May of London, merchant - Son of Thomas May, to whom I served my time'. In addition, he left £75,000 to his goddaughter and others, an annuity of £40,000 per annum to Mrs Elizabeth Burt "who resided with me for many years", as well as £13,000 to other servants and two further bequests of £40,000, one of which was to his apothecary. The house became home to Joseph until it passed to his son John. Joseph's sister, Margaret, and her mother took a tenancy of No 4 Tavistock Street, Bedford Square, on 20th April, 1782. The house was associated with the family for another fifty years. Joseph also "determined to purchase some pleasant country residence" and acquired Hale Park, between Fordingbridge and Salisbury, in 1783, together with 3,000 acres, for a total sum of £43,600. The house had been built by Thomas Archer around 1720. By 1793 it had been altered to Joseph's satisfaction. The family also owned a town home at 80 Gower Street, Bedford Square.

Joseph and Mary had ten children, five boys and five girls. Two sons were involved in the family business: John who occupied Old Friars on Richmond Green, when it passed to his mother, and William, the youngest who spent much of his time overseas. The first-born son, Joseph, inherited Hale Manor and became head of the family upon his father's death.

John May was a merchant by profession, but he also became involved in business as a financier and insurance agent. He was for many years a Director of the Equitable Assurance Company.16 His circle of friends and associates was very wide. He was a benefactor of Robert Southey (born in Wine Street, Bristol on 12th August 1774)17 and also of John Taylor Coleridge amongst others. John Taylor, a nephew of Samuel Taylor Coleridge, was born, according to his father's entry in the register of Ottery St. Mary, "about 11 o'clock in the forenoon of 21 October 1772".

Rev. George Coleridge

Before John's first year was over, he returned to England with his parents in 1775. From 1784 he was educated at Newcome's Academy in Hackney. His tutor, George Coleridge, became a lifelong friend. He had a good classical education but did not proceed to university. After he had left Newcome's Academy, George Coleridge continued to advise him, suggesting in 1793 that he should not read Thucydides, "without a good Scholia".18 John May became godfather to George's son, christened George May Coleridge, at Ottery St Mary on 27th November 1798. From this friendship he met James Coleridge (the Colonel), who was to become another close friend, as well as Samuel Taylor Coleridge.

Surviving correspondence with George Coleridge commences from November, 1792, at which date John was seventeen and had just left Newcome's Academy. In 1793 Coleridge speaks of the "infant state of our intimacy".19 John's younger brother, Arthur Stert May, aged 13, was also at Newcome's under the tuition of George Coleridge. His elder brother, Thomas Charles May, had been similarly educated. William

Hale House, Hampshire by Thomas Boyes.

Coleridge, a Greek scholar and also a master at Newcome's, commented at the time on John's "well directed studies".[20]

John sailed back to Lisbon early in 1793 to learn the family business from the house of his uncle, Thomas Coppendale. He worked alongside John Worthington, "a good sort of young man"[21] who had been admitted to the 'Factory' on 20 January, 1803[22] whilst living in Rio de Janeiro. John Worthington remained in the family business for some years. There is no record of John May having been admitted to the 'Factory'.

On 7th May, 1793, John's brother, Joseph, wrote to him at his Uncle Thomas Coppendale's house in Lisbon. He told him how pleased he was that John was happy and he offered brotherly advice on the company he should seek: "I am sure your own observation and good sense must ere this have pointed out to you the advantages you possess in the conversation and friendship of Mrs Burn, and you will excuse the zealous anxiety of a brother when I conjure you to study her with attention, and to endeavour to catch from her that art of pleasing which carries such weight with it in every affair of the world, and without which the most estimable qualities a man can possess are often times of little or no avail to him; Mrs Walpole too, though not so eminently accomplished as her

16

aunt, is a lady from whom much in this way may be learnt, especially by a young man on whom it is natural to suppose that the circumstances of youth and beauty will have some effect."[23]

William and Jane Burn were also attached to the British Factory at Lisbon. William had been admitted in 1772. They had returned to England by 1806 and occupied a house at 7, St George Street, Hanover Square. In 1815 they moved to Wick House on Richmond Hill, a house built for Sir Joshua Reynolds. It is situated next door to The Wick that later became the home of John May and his family. Jane Burn was sister-in-law to Richard Stert, the Lisbon wine merchant. Some years later John went into partnership with the Stert family and experienced acrimony from the association. Fanny Stert, Richard's daughter, married John May's brother Joseph in 1797. The Burns were also related to the Walpole family, as Fanny's sister, Sophia, had married Horace Walpole's cousin, the Hon. Robert Walpole, Ambassador at the Court of Portugal.[24]

Joseph advised John on the qualities of Mr Burn and Mr Walpole. With regard to Thomas Coppendale he wrote: "What you say about my uncle has been perfectly well received by my good father and mother who would be sorry were you to discontinue that frankness they have too long been used to, so that you need not feel yourself uneasy on that head, but you need not despair of acquiring his confidence, time and good management will no doubt offer it, however I shall add nothing more as I fancy my father has written to you fully upon this subject. I am sure you must be much pleased with my good-natured aunt Coppendale."[25]

In a later letter there is a description of Thomas: "Rough he is no doubt, and of severe manners, but study him and his temper, and my word for it, the longer you know him the better you will be pleased with him."[26]

Back home Joseph May carried out extensive building works at Hale Manor. Workmen were on site for eight years. The roof was replaced and lowered around 1790. On one of the timbers is carved the name 'J Pope 1791'. The Popes moved from Poole in Dorset to settle in Downton and worked on the building for the entire construction period. Farm buildings close to the house were removed and a west wing added.[27] John's father, Joseph, proudly wrote to him on 12 August, 1793, with a description of the work being undertaken: "You would find much done since you were here. The Stucco of the house is nearly finished, & looks exceeding well, the columns are up - the old farm & all its history

17

taken down, & the ground properly levelled, which forms a beautiful appearance from the Veranda & the Dining Parlour & perfectly satisfies me. - Fields work has all been very well done - the veranda on the South Side which looks on the new Flower garden & Greenhouse finished & the pavement placed, the Stone Balustrading up, but not yet the iron railing - In the house the flooring quite finished - the great staircase now beginning to be put up - and in about 10 days time I expect to have the Drawing Room, & my two Rooms finished so far as to have the windows fixed, & ready to inhabit without however the circumstance of either being painted - indeed we defer all that work till the winter or next spring, that we may not be poisoned. Now for farming affairs - Our hay harvest has been good and well saved - Our Corn harvest is just begun, and promises to be plentiful with us, and over the whole Country - I wish we had such good accounts of your Harvests and Vintages - also interesting to those concerned in your trade, and in the welfare of the human race."[28]

Today the staircase in the central hall is just as imposing as when Joseph had it built. It ascends around three walls of the hall to a galleried landing under an overhead light. The drawing room and two rooms described take in the views to the west of the house, the church and the River Avon.

Delighted with his son's progress Joseph added "I am pleased with the account you give me of the manner in which you pass your time at Lisbon, and that you find Worthington a good sort of young man, willing to give you assistance by his instructions in the way of your business." Referring to John's old tutor George Coleridge he commented "Before we left town, I called on Arthur, (John's brother) & found him well, & it will be a satisfaction to you to hear, as it was to me, from Mr Coleridge himself, that he did not mean to quit Mr Newcome's School. He spoke much of you & of his friendship for you, & to give you his kind Remembrance."[29]

Despite his assurances to Joseph, by November, 1794, George Coleridge had left Newcome's to become Schoolmaster and Chaplain Priest of King's School, Ottery St Mary, Devon. He told John how unhappy he had been for thirteen years. He put his perseverance down to his "duties as a Son and Brother".[30]

A good family friend and financier, Batt Forbes, was staying at Hale in 1793 whilst recovering from an illness and apparently eating the family out of house and home. The family's friendship was later to be poorly repaid by a bad debt. Miss Forbes was a frequent companion to Aunt Margaret and John's sisters at the turn of the century, in London, Richmond and Hale.

George and James Coleridge's brother, the poet Samuel Taylor Coleridge, met Robert Southey in June 1794 while he was on a walking tour to North Wales. In August Samuel went to Bristol and was introduced by Southey to Mrs Fricker and her daughters. Southey was shortly to be engaged to Edith Fricker. As well as intellectual companions and future brothers-in-law they became closely joined in the bond of Pantisocracy and dreamed of establishing a Utopian society on the banks of the Susquehanna River.

Thomas Poole wrote the following contemporary account of Pantisocracy: "Twelve gentlemen of good education and liberal principles are to embark with twelve ladies in April next. Previous to their leaving this country they are to have as much intercourse as possible, in order to ascertain each other's dispositions, and firmly to settle every regulation for the government of their future conduct. Their opinion was that they should fix themselves at - I do not recollect the place, but somewhere in a delightful part of the new back settlements; that each man should labour two or three hours a day, the produce of which labour would, they imagine, be more than sufficient to support the colony. As Adam Smith observes that there is not above one productive man in twenty, they argue that if each laboured the twentieth part of time, it would produce enough to satisfy their wants. The produce of their industry is to be laid up in common for the use of all; and a good library of books is to be collected, and their leisure hours to be spent in study, liberal discussions, and the education of their children.....The regulations relating to the females strike them as the most difficult; whether the marriage contract shall be dissolved if agreeable to one or both parties, and many other circumstances, are not yet determined The employments of the women are to be the care of infant children, and other occupations suited to their strength; at the same time the greatest attention is to be paid to the cultivation of their minds. Every one is to enjoy his own religious and political opinions, provided they do not encroach on the rules previously made, which rules, it is unnecessary to add, must in some measure be regulated by the laws of the state which includes the district in which they settle. They calculate that each gentleman providing £125 will be sufficient to carry the scheme into execution. Finally, every individual is at liberty, whenever he pleases, to withdraw from the society."[31]

In August, 1794, Robert Southey and Samuel Taylor Coleridge went on a walking tour to Nether Stowey, Thomas Poole's home. Two years later Coleridge rented a cottage there where he lived for three years and in 1797 William and Dorothy Wordsworth moved to Alfoxden, outside the nearby village of Holford.

Pantisocracy required that the men should be married and Coleridge, partly persuaded by Southey, and partly to fulfil this requirement, married Sara Fricker in Bristol on 4th October, 1795. Sara was the sister of Robert Southey's fiancee, Edith. They in turn were secretly married on 14th November at St Mary Redcliffe. Whereas their union was apparently happy and lasted until Edith's death in 1837, Coleridge's marriage to Sara was not to last. Edith, concealing her wedding ring by wearing it around her neck, moved to the Cottle's house where she lived, largely under her maiden name, until Southey returned from his first journey to Portugal, where he met John May. Southey was twenty-two years old. He had gone to visit his uncle, the Reverend Herbert Hill, who had been chaplain to the British Factory in Oporto since 1774.[32] Southey and May remained friends and correspondents for the remainder of Southey's life. John May provided finance for Southey's early works.

By the end of 1794 Joseph's work on Hale was almost complete and he was busy furnishing the mansion to an extent that apparently concerned his son John, even though he was far away in Lisbon. Joseph tried to pacify his son by writing on 26th October: "You rather, I think, suspect that I am stripping Old Richmond to decorate and comfort Hale. I have too many obligations to that old Mansion to see it ill, and though I take some Books from the A, B & C I shall still have the shelves well furnished for a Winter or a Spring's reading - Indeed I always find myself much at home there, and if Hale has her charms and is a favourite Mistress, Richmond is a beloved wife."[33]

Around July 1795, John sent George Coleridge a present of superior wine from Portugal and received a letter thanking him and noting that George had heard that John was considering returning to England.[34] Late in 1795 John made a business trip to Spain. However, it seems that by the time he was introduced to Robert Southey in 1796, he

John May. 1798.
from Robert Southey.

only twelve copies were printed in this size.
R.S.

JOAN OF ARC,

AN

EPIC POEM.

BY

ROBERT SOUTHEY.

TWO VOLUMES.

SECOND EDITION.

Title page, First Edition, 1798. (printed for Joseph Cottle)
(By courtesy of The Wordsworth Trust, Dove Cottage, Grasmere, Cumbria.)

had finally decided that Portugal was not the place for him. His father meanwhile had been working to place him in partnership with Thomas Coppendale. John returned to England on 21st May, 1796. Joseph died the same year on 31st October at Hale. Robert Southey wrote an epitaph which John thought "might be fitly placed upon his tomb: "The quiet virtues of domestic life were his, who lies below: therefore his paths were paths of pleasantness, & in that hour, when all the perishable joys of earth desert the desolate heart, he had the hope, the sure & certain hope of Joy in Heaven."[35]

In January, 1797, George Coleridge's brother, Edward, moved to Ottery St Mary, where he was to establish a private school at Rock House which was formed out of the stables of "the Great House". John May made a social visit to the Coleridges at Ottery in the spring of 1797. He was made very welcome and George advised him in general terms regarding a family crest or motto. John adopted a crest for which his granddaughter obtained formal recognition after his death.

George Coleridge's son was born in 1797. In June he asked John May to be godfather using his "friend's surname between George and Coleridge". By December John's younger brother, William Henry, aged twelve, was at King's School. George appears to have adopted a paternal role towards him as he sent regular reports of William's progress throughout his education at King's.[36]

In June, 1797, Robert Southey wrote to John May from Christchurch telling him that he had begun a tragedy on the martyrdom of Joan of Arc.[37] His writing continued through the year and John visited him at Burton in the summer.[38] In December, after the sale of his mother's Bristol house and before he moved to lodgings in Lambs Conduit Street, Southey stayed with John May at Richmond. They both took a great interest in humanitarian matters, John May foregoing sugar in the hope of discouraging the slave trade. John opened an office in London where he met beggars and learned their history.[39] On December 24, 1797, Robert Southey wrote to his brother, Thomas, setting out, in some detail, a scheme he and John had discussed for the setting up of a charitable institution. It was to employ poor convalescent patients to become self-sufficient by gardening and making nets, baskets, matting and sheeting, any surplus being sold - "Six hours' labour is all that will be required from the strongest persons."[40]

At Bath, in the spring of 1798, Southey investigated an old charity for John and discovered that thirteen paupers were supported upon a foundation that had increased in value to £100,000, and that well-nigh £5000 a year went "to no one knew who."[41] He wrote some verses entitled, "The Complaints of the Poor", which he sent to John in July.[42] In the same year 'Joan of Arc' was published and he despatched a copy to John from Bristol writing on 5th May: "You will I hope receive Joan of Arc on Tuesday morning".[43] The two volumes inscribed by hand: 'John May, 1798, from Robert Southey' are now in the library of the Wordsworth Trust in Grasmere. Later in the year in November, Southey accepted John's invitation to stay with him at Richmond, but declined a further offer of financial aid.[44]

John did however provide financial and mercantile help to James Coleridge (The Colonel), Lt. Col. of the Exmouth and Sidmouth Volunteers and for many years aide-de-camp for General Simcoe who was then commander of the Western Division. This was much appreciated and another friendship was forged. He also helped Edward Coleridge financially over a period of years.[45]

During 1797 John was considering asking Charlotte Hair, a young lady he had met in Lisbon, to marry him and he sought his friend George's advice. Whilst George reminded John of the apostle Paul's words of its being "better to marry than burn" there seems to be a note of caution in his advice and shortly after he "hopes that marriage will meet his expectations."[46] George Coleridge received a gift of Anderson's British Poets in June 1799, handsomely bound in 13 Volumes large octavo. They were sent from Stockdale's in Piccadilly and were the second set of valuable books that he had received since moving to Devon. Both sets had been delivered anonymously. Although he wrote in vain to Stockdales to ask who his benefactor was, it seems likely that the books were sent by John May who was an avid bibliophile.[47] In the same month Southey had written to him asking if he could obtain a copy of Anquetil Du Perron's Zendavesta, "It is not easily met with, but perhaps your bookseller might meet with a copy."[48] Southey made frequent requests for books.

In September, Samuel Taylor Coleridge and his wife were staying at Ottery whilst Southey visited George Coleridge. Writing to John he records: "I have now seen George Coleridge; his brother and you had taught me to respect him. In many things he reminds me of you; there is the resemblance that two persons who have lived much together, and

23

Old Friars, Richmond Green

with attached affections, bear to each other . . . I have just learnt that you do not visit Devonshire, I, however, have the expectation of seeing you in Hampshire during the winter. George Coleridge has been very friendly towards me, and I feel that his opinion of me had been influenced by you."[49] He was able to thank John for obtaining "the Zendavesta" for him.

The turn of the century was eventful for the lives of Samuel Taylor Coleridge, Robert Southey, John May and the Wordsworths. Coleridge met Sarah Hutchinson (Wordsworth's future sister-in-law) at Sockburn in Yorkshire, fell in love with her and destroyed any peace he had previously enjoyed with his wife. Southey became increasingly worried about his heart and health. Writing to John on 18th February, 1800, he mentioned his concerns and spoke of visiting Portugal again. He sailed with Edith in April, 1800, returning in June, 1801. Before sailing he had written a detailed letter to John setting out all his arrangements and what needed to be done: "First, as to pecuniary matters. Reviewing, of course must be suspended, and I have for some months, ceased writing for the newspaper, owing to inability from ill-health. The loss is not less than a hundred a year . . . my annual income remains 160*l.*, which you will receive quarterly for me, and to which amount I will draw on you. There will be also from ten to twenty pounds due from the "Critical Review," which I shall direct be paid to you. I shall send over my "Thalaba" for publication in Lisbon; this will assuredly, though I reserve the copyright of the after editions, produce 100l."[50]

Whilst John had made arrangements for Southey to obtain money from his Uncle Coppendale in Lisbon if needed, Southey's letters contain frequent references to his drawing money on John. During his stay in Portugal Southey used his contacts with May and his business partners. He obtained books from Mr Worthington in June, 1800, and wrote in September to say that he had had no need to obtain money from May's partner, Mr Coppendale.[51] On 19th March, before leaving, he had asked what was the best method of conveying or receiving money: "Should I take bills on Lisbon? Or draw from thence?" On the eve of sailing April 12th, he sent John a draft for fifty pounds and told him that, "Whatever money you may receive for me shall be paid to you, without any trouble on your part. I have thought it prudent to insure my baggage & my Uncles orders for £100 - as privateers swarm so on the Spanish coast."[52]

Thomas and Rose Dea took the two Miss Livius girls for a second visit to Hale Manor in the summer and on 13th November, 1799. John announced his engagement to Susanna Frances Livius. Susan, as she was called, was a granddaughter of Peter Lewis Livius, the King of Prussia's Envoy to the Court of Lisbon. Her father Peter who died in July, 1795, had been the Chief Justice of Quebec. She was baptised on 27th September, 1767, at Portsmouth, Rockingham, New Hampshire. Southey sent his congratulations on 29th November, rejoicing in his friend's happiness and reflecting on his own.[53] On 12th December, 1799, John and Susanna were married at St Giles-in-the-Fields, London. Brother Joseph and his wife made their excuses due to the distance from Hale.[54]

The following month William Wordsworth and his sister Dorothy moved to Dove Cottage, Grasmere, and were followed to Cumberland in July, 1800 by Samuel and Sara Coleridge, who arrived to live in Greta Hall, Keswick.

At the turn of the year, John wrote to George Coleridge on behalf of a friend who sought a place at Ottery for his son. George replied saying that his school numbered twenty-five boys, a total he might reduce but never increase. He had a waiting list of about fifteen, "many of them the

Brothers of the Boys now with me." It was, he felt, improbable that he could find a place for the son of John's friend for at least three years "if I had no other objection to your proposal".[55] He commented also on intelligence that John had provided regarding Samuel Taylor's movements: "I did not know that my Brother Sam was in London. I am not much in his confidence and cannot ever guess where he is to be found. I feel however most grateful to you for your unwearied attention to my Family." Early in 1800 the two men exchanged miniature portraits. George Coleridge sent his to 80 Gower Street, Bedford Square, where John's mother was living.[56]

As well as financial adviser John also acted as agent to Southey. In a post-script to a letter dated May, 1800, Southey wrote: "Forgive me if I trouble you as my agent with some commissions. I want for my Uncle a silver hunting watch price 5 guineas - it is for Manuel. Wartons Essay on Pope & Wartons History of Poetry. The books of course must be bound. - They must be directed to my Uncle."[57]

John and Susan had set up their home at 'Old Friars' on Richmond Green, but they spent some time with Aunt Margaret in Tavistock Street.

John undertook a mercantile venture with his brother Joseph and Mr Menet in the autumn. They entered into a partnership with a Mr Duval who invested the equivalent of one million pounds in today's values into the existing business allowing it to expand. John and Susan's first daughter, also Susan, was born on 26th September, 1800, and baptised at St. Mary Magdalene, Richmond on 1st October. The impending birth had caused Southey some anxiety which he expressed in a letter to John written on 1st September from Cintra: "Your information in the last letter will make me tremblingly anxious for it shall be time to expect it."[58] and on 29th October from Lisbon: "Your half-letter was more welcome than any full-grown one that has reached me since my arrival in Portugal . . . The birth of your little girl forces on me the knowledge how far I am advanced in my own life-journey."[59]

Little Susan died on 12th February, 1801. Aunt Margaret recorded the sad events in her diary: "1801 - Feb - My Nephew John & Susan being returned from Hale they brought their child with them."

"1801 - Feb 7th - They returned to Richmond"

"1801 - Feb 10th - Tuesday . . . John came to town but in consequence of a letter from Susan informing him the Child was in danger he returned at ten at night & at one in the morning a Chaise came here for him as the Child was thought to be dying - "

1801 - Feb 12th - "I went to Richmond . . . we found that the Dear Child had dyed that morning & poor John & Susan in great affliction."[60] She also recorded the elopement of Charlotte Livius, John's sister- in-law, with a Mr Digby in December and her marriage the same month. The initial scandal was forgiven with the passage of time. On 6th August, 1801, Aunt Margaret set out on a family tour of Devon with her nephews and nieces. Having spent a month on their tour she noted a visit to the Coleridges when George was unwell at the dinner table :-

"Sept 6th - we proceeded thro Exeter to Ottery St Mary"

"Sept 7th- We slept at Mr Coleridges"

John May had powerful contacts in the financial world. In 1801 George Coleridge wrote to him asking if the grandson of F. Baring, of the banking family, was still interested in attending his school as he was on his list and could soon be received.[61]

Samuel Taylor Coleridge's letters to Southey became increasingly enthusiastic in his praise of Greta Hall and he tried several times to convince him to join his family there. He wrote describing the house and situation:. "Our house stands on a low hill, the whole front of which is one field and an enormous garden, nine tenths of which is a nursery garden. Behind the house is an orchard, and a small wood on a steep slope, at the foot of which flows the River Greta, which winds round and catches the evening lights in the front of the house. In front we have a giant's camp - an encamped army of tent like mountains, which by an inverted arch gives a view of another vale. On our right the lovely vale and the wedge-shaped lake of Bassenthwaite; and on our left Derwentwater and Lodore full in view, and the fantastic mountains of Borrowdale. Behind us the massy Skiddaw, smooth, green, high, with two chasms and a tent-like ridge in the larger. A fairer scene you have not seen in all your wanderings. Without going from our own grounds, we have all that can please a human being . . .

"The house is full twice as large as we want: it hath more rooms in it than Allfoxen: you might have a bedroom, parlour, study, &c., &c., and there would always be rooms to spare for your or my visitors. In short, for situation and convenience - and when I mention the name of Wordsworth, for society of men of intellect - I know no place in which you and Edith would find yourselves so well suited."[62]

Robert and Edith Southey returned to England on 6th July, 1801.

Southey was in debt to John May as he recognised in July: "I am anxious to know my account with you. It will leave me deeply in your debt, my spirits are heavily depressed - nothing but ill tidings greet me. I have purchased health by running in debt."[63] He visited the Coleridges at Greta Hall, Keswick, in September but was not impressed and compared the Lakes to the rivers of Portugal, complained of the cold weather and longed to be back in Cintra again. In October he went on a brief tour in North Wales. During the tour he was offered a job as assistant to Mr Corry, Chancellor of the Exchequer in Dublin, at a salary of £200 a year with a similar sum for travelling. He accepted, returned to Keswick, packed, left his wife with her sister and went to Dublin. In his loneliness he missed the lakes and mountains.[64] His work took him to London where he saw John. By July, 1802 his work for Mr Corry had finished.

Storm clouds were gathering over John's business. Reports from Portugal brought ever more gloomy portents of war. His good friends tried to comfort him and felt he would weather the storm, "albeit with some derangement."[65]

On 8th March, 1802, Aunt Margaret recorded in her diary - "John May's little boy born the 8th"[66]

1802 - 1822

John May (the younger) known as 'Johnny' was born at 'Old Friars' Richmond Green on 8th March, 1802, and baptised at St Mary Magdalene on March 31st. Rev George Coleridge wrote congratulating John and offered to be a godfather. The offer was not taken up on this occasion but he stayed with the Mays at Breamore and Hale during the spring where the two men discussed John's possible return to Lisbon - a plan that did not materialise.

Robert and Edith Southey were expecting a child at the same time and considered moving to Richmond. In the early summer Southey wrote to his friends, John Rickman, Grosvenor Bedford and Miss Barker, informing them that he had commissioned John May to find him a house in Richmond by Michaelmas: "But I hope I am coming to live near London - not in its filth. If John May can find me a good snug house about Richmond, there I will go." [67&68]

He also wrote to John: "After weighing maturely and considerately the relative advantages of the only three dwelling places to which there exists any motive of preference - Norwich, Bristol, and the neighbourhood of London - I decidedly prefer the last, because it gives me access to public and private libraries, and places me within reach of the booksellers, with whom I may from time to time engage in works of obscure profit. The neighbourhood of London means your neighbourhood, for the convenience of finding a house, and the comfort of living in it when found. The nearness of many acquaintances is a matter of luxury, but one friend within a half-hours walk is among the necessaries of life."[69]

The Southey's daughter, Margaret Edith, was born on 1st September, 1802. John offered to be a godfather and, on 5th September, Southey wrote thanking him for his offer and accepted it gladly. He still needed to settle his family and thought he had arranged a sensible move to Greta Hall where he could occupy part of the house, furnished, for twenty guineas a year, which was half the London rates.[70] This offer did not materialise and he went to Wales instead, then on to Bristol and London.

The two men continued their correspondence sharing news about their young children. Southey wrote in November, "Young John, I trust, goes on well, and will soon begin to find what legs were made for."[71] Later: "I have not yet thanked you for Margaret's wardrobe . . . Edith joins me in remembrances to Mrs May, I cannot wish your little boy to be better than my Margaret - who is all health & activity & good spirits & good humour."[72]

Sara Coleridge was born on 23rd December, 1802. She was the daughter of Samuel Taylor and his wife Sara and was destined to meet and break Johnny May's heart some twenty years later.[73]

1803 was a bad year for John May. His second son, Richard, was born on 11th February but died soon after. George Coleridge agreed to be a sponsor but could not be present at the baptism asking John to select some one for his proxy but writing that he would "contribute the necessary sum for the nurses as is usual in your neighbourhood or I shall not think that I have been a Godfather."[74] Richard died on 21st February so George never met him.

There were great fears for Susan's health. Aunt Margaret's diary records:

Feb 11th "My Niece Susan May brought to bed of a Boy."
Feb 14th "heard that my Niece Susan was dangerously ill."
Feb, 18th "My Sisters and Nieces arrived at Richmond."

29

Feb 21st "John's Infant died."

Feb 28th "We had bad accounts of Susan."[75]

John's brother, Joseph, wrote from Hale Manor several times in February congratulating him on the birth, expressing hopes that "our beloved Susan is now out of danger, & that all your fears on her account are over" and requesting frequent accounts.[76] The improvement in Susan's health was tempered by the loss of her baby. Joseph wrote again: "The continued good accounts we receive of your good Susan have given the most heartfelt satisfaction both to Fanny & myself & although our joy for her recovery has been somewhat damped by the loss you have both of you recently sustained in the decease of your poor infant, we must beg of you to reflect what a mercy has been accorded to you in the sparing your beloved companion . . . & we send kisses in abundance to that noble fellow little John." Robert Southey also expressed his concern for further news from Bristol.[77]

In March John planned to move from Old Friars to Marsh Gate also in Richmond and George was relieved that Mrs May is "so much better as to be excited about moving into another room."[78] Her well being remained a major cause for concern through to April. By this time John and his brother, Joseph, were experiencing more financial difficulties in the family business with debts that remained unpaid. Southey again wrote to him from Bristol: "I need not say that your last letter gave me great pain, but it was less than I apprehended from your long silence & your mourning wafer, the black wafer had made me so fully believe the worst, that the intelligence of your other losses heavy as they are, came like a light evil. I hope however you will yet recover more than you seemed to expect . . . Margaret is growing a very fine little girl, her mother still suckles her, we are all well. Your next I hope will bring me as good an account of your family I hope - a fairer prospect of retrieving the very heavy losses which you have sustained from the dishonesty of others."[79]

The May family spent the summer months recuperating in Weymouth and at Hale Manor whilst John made the journey to and from London on business staying sometimes at the coaching inn at Hartford Bridge. Southey frequently passed copies of his works to John for his opinions and he found time to read *Thalaba* for which Robert was appropriately grateful.[80]

Circumstances were now difficult enough for John to remind his brother, Joseph, of an outstanding sum of money owed to him. Joseph wrote back: "The balance upon your account with me is indeed very greatly against me." Batt Forbes owed the brothers money and John was helping Joseph's finances from the profits of the Lisbon trading house. Joseph told his brother he was prepared to undertake any other employment, "should such employment prove congenial to my station in life".[81] John required capital and disposed of Old Friars moving to Marsh Gate. By November, 1803, he was settled there with his family.

Robert Southey still hankered after a move to Richmond and John May was closely involved in the matter. Whilst apparently in negotiation for a property he wrote to John on 5th May: "When we talked with Mr Phillips I understood that if the fixtures were taken by appraisement the house was to be let much lower, & this be dwelt upon, but the £40 was to be the rent including the fixtures. I am so sure of this that I suspect you have used the word by mistake instead of furniture . . . Your next I hope will tell me that the business is settled, & that I am to consider myself as your neighbour in futuro."[82] Mr Phillips was Jacob Phillips, brother-in-law of George Coleridge and a conveyancer known to both John May and Robert Southey. Negotiations continued through to July and Southey wrote again on 20th: "The more I think and talk of the house at Richmond the more I am disposed to have the bargain concluded; that is, if the inside be tolerably convenient, which there should seem little reason to doubt. The taxes, indeed, are very high, but they must bear nearly the same proportion to rent everywhere in the neighbourhood of London. If you can get sight of the premises, and find them comfortably habitable, as doubtless they must be, I shall be very glad to take it for a term, and have every thing settled. The sooner the better; that, if any unforeseen circumstance prevents us from getting this, we may lose no time in looking out for another."[83]

Southey's dream of a house close to his friend in Richmond was never to be fulfilled as in August his daughter Margaret died and was buried on 23rd. The heartbroken parents moved north to Keswick almost immediately arriving at Greta Hall on 7th September, 1803. He wanted Edith to be with her sister Sara and her young child to try and "graft her into the wound, while it is still fresh." He informed John: "I shall, with all speed set off for Cumberland."[84] Edith quickly became pregnant again and on December 24th he told John his news with slight apprehension: "You will be glad to hear that in the course of the spring I shall perhaps be once more a father & yet I know not whether I am glad to inform you."[85]

Through 1803 and 1804 a wave of patriotism spread over England with talk of a French invasion and an embargo on all ships bound for Spain or Portugal. Southey passed on the gossip to his friend Wynn: "Rickman tells me there will be no army sent to Portugal; that it is understood the French may overrun it at pleasure, and that we then lay open Brazil and Spanish America."[86] He told John, "All Bristol is up in arms and volunteering - cool sport for the dog-days . . . All this, however, is very necessary. A few weeks more, and England will be in a formidable state of preparation, if they arm the people as is talked of." John May was "a soldier by this time" he observed in September and added, "I, too, shall fire away at Bonaparte, and perhaps hit him, for he reads the 'Morning Post'."[87] George Coleridge also noted on 24th December: "I am told that you and your Brother William are in the ranks. This is like yourselves."[88]

Southey and Wordsworth were involved: "Great news at Keswick: a firing heard off the Isle of Man at four o'clock in the morning yesterday! The French are a coming, a coming, a coming - and what care we? We, who have eighteen volunteers, and an apothecary at their head!"[89] Wordsworth thought the numbers pitiful at Keswick and pointed out that "at Grasmere, we have turned out almost to a Man."

By November, 1803, John's business in Portugal was badly effected. Southey wrote encouraging him: "What you say of your own affairs grieves me deeply. I have no consolation to offer perhaps the evil may be averted. - God prevent it! Yet at the worst you are a man prepared for the change, & a mind of Xtian fortitude extracts not only consolation but even a shield of joy from endurance." He reminded John that his relatives had the wealth and will to help him through the bad times.[90]

Edith May Southey was born on 1st May, 1804, and John was once again appointed as godfather. In the same year Aunt Margaret recorded the birth of another child to John and Susan': "Susan May brought to bed of a daughter Sep 11th who was named immediately Mary Charlotte."[91] She was baptised at Richmond on 15th September, 1804. She was destined in later life to subject her family to shame and scandal.

Joseph wrote an interesting domestic family letter to John in February, 1805: "Let me first begin with Fanny's business, the paper I am to copy for her runs thus - 'If sugar is cheap John will be kind enough to

32

order for - 100 lb of common breakfast sugar and 50 lb of the best double refined for ourselves, and 50 lb for the use of the kitchen and the Servants, this to be the loaf sugar and will like wise order 100 lb of moist sugar. That sugar be dear and a probability of them becoming cheaper half the quantity of each will do for the present. I likewise wish for one qr of cwt of green tea that used to be sold for eight shillings per lb. 4 lb of gunpowder, & 12 lb of common tea for servants; all the tea to be purchased of Twining"[92]

By April, 1805, the debt owed by Forbes, together with interest was £1144.12.11d and remained unpaid. Joseph wrote to Jack Forbes, the son, who promised payment in 4 to 6 months. The debt was, he said, seriously "impeding John May in his mercantile concerns."[93]

Throughout 1805 John and Robert Southey exchanged letters with news of their children and thoughts on the wars. John commented again on Southey's work in July, this time *Madoc*. At the same time he was asked to obtain *Beausobre's Histoire de Manicheisme* which Robert could not obtain "for want of catalogues".[94] John suffered with an inflammation of the eyes to the extent that for a while he had to have complete rest. This was a recurring problem in his life.

In the summer the May family went on holiday together to Hampshire and Aunt Margaret wrote in her diary:

1805 - July 6th - "I went to Marsh Gate where I remained till the 11th. When I set out for Egham Lodge & on the 15th set out from thence to Hale where I arrived at eight o'clock the same night - Several dinner partys at home & abroad, & the 25th we all set out in the afternoon for Southampton where we met my Neice & Nephew May & their family, we slept there & the next morning at ten o'clock sailed for the Isle of Wight where we arrived in an hour & 40 minutes at Cowes - We remained at Cowes till the 13rd of August & returned to Hale, we were seven hours on our voyage from Cowes to Southampton. The Month we spent at Cowes was very agreeable, the weather was fine & we went to see all the places worth notice in the island - the Undercliffe, Shanklin, Sea Cottage, Sr Nash Groses etc., I bathed 7 times in the Warm bath which I think was of service."[95]

Susan was expecting again. In November, 1805, she gave birth to another daughter who was baptised in Richmond and named Susanna Louisa. Robert Southey immediately sent his congratulations to John: "I do therefore heartily congratulate you on the birth of another child, looking upon a large family as a blessing, though the state of society too often makes it otherwise. I fear I have little prospect of another myself."[96] John, in his turn, still took his duties as a godfather seriously regularly sending gifts to Edith that were duly appreciated. Robert wrote to Lt Southey on 22nd May, 1806 that his daughter has had "some fine clothes from her god-father John May" and to John on 18th June telling him, "My daughter was so delighted with the new gown which Mrs May sent her, that I thought it expedient to inform her that new gowns were among the pomps and vanities of this wicked world; a warning which, as you may perhaps suppose, has not made her a whit the less proud of it."[97]

Southey's relationship with his brother-in-law Samuel had not improved. He told John in October, 1806 that they were still waiting for his arrival although he had been in England for three months and the few letters he had sent were written in the "very worst mood of despondency, as if he never wrote till he had exhausted his whole stock of spirits in conversation."[98]

John's financial position continued to deteriorate as did the plight of the Forbes family. Aunt Margaret's diary records the "distressing intelligence" from Hale in 1806 that affected her health. It seems that B. Forbes never discharged the debt and brought shame and ruin on his family. Joseph wrote to John in February, 1807: "I am truly concerned at what was stated by you in your last letter to my mother respecting the Forbes family; most heartily do I lament their misfortunes and most sincerely the miserable situation in which all of them, but more especially the poor innocent females of the family, are placed, you have done perfectly right in placing my name and that of Tom for the sums mentioned in your letter by way of subscription . . . for I can never forget that they have been amongst my earliest friends and although the men have been faulty, and most generously so, I cannot for the soul of me accuse their hearts or intentions, or at any rate at present think of anything but their calamities: remember however when I say this I allude to the young men, old Mr Forbes - I neither wish to see, to hear of, or if possible to think of again, I cannot but consider him the author and the uncorrected continuer of his families misfortunes."[99]

Joseph sent his best wishes to old Mrs Forbes. He agreed to any scheme which John could devise to provide the welfare needed whilst he bemoaned the state of his own financial situation: "It is a dreadful thing to have the wish but not the power to do good, when accompanied by this sad reflection that the power has been lost by ones own faulty impudence."

In 1807 Rev George Coleridge fell out with his brother Samuel Taylor. George had invited him to stay at Ottery. Samuel wrote to him on 2nd April, 1807, saying he was prepared to move to Ottery and help George with his school if he so wished even though this would mean his leaving Wordsworth. In the same letter he announced his intention of living apart from his wife but said they would come together to Ottery for appearance sake. George replied immediately, He was horrified at the news and told Samuel that his accommodation was full. Samuel should not leave his wife and, "It is necessary for me now to tell you that I have made my final arrangements for giving up the School.... so that I cannot offer you to take the children under my care." He counselled him, "For God's sake strive to put on some fortitude and do nothing rashly." George Coleridge was so upset that he told all his Ottery family and the word circulated. Samuel wrote to friends and associates in 1807 complaining of his harsh treatment by his brother who had invited him to Ottery and that Col Coleridge's "eldest son (a mere youth) had informed Mr King that he should not call me (his Uncle) for that 'The Family' had resolved not to receive me."[100] Some four years later John May was to play a part in reconciling Samuel and his nephews.

The May family's financial fortunes continued to decline. John's mother's will had been written shortly after his father's death in 1796. It devised the Hale estate to the elder son Joseph, £10,000 each to Tom and John, £8,000 each to Arthur and William, and £10,000 to each of her four daughters. The residue was to be divided amongst the five sons. In the ensuing ten years it became clear that the provision made for Joseph was inadequate to maintain him at Hale in the position of 'head of the family'. The value of the real property had been increased by the redemption of Land Tax and the purchase of a farm, both paid for from the residuary estate. Joseph had, however, incurred debts of over £32,300 to his mother. At the same time his mother's expenditure from her husband's death until her own, exceeded her income by some £23,100. Mr Lewis, a solicitor employed by John on his mother's behalf, had relieved her of £2,000 and she had given Joseph a house at Bramshaw worth some £1,400. With the agreement of all concerned the will was revised on 3rd August, 1807, in Joseph's favour. He was to inherit all his mother's property in Hampshire, Wiltshire and Childe Okeford, Dorset, together with a farm in Rodmersham, Kent, various Fee Farm rents in the City of London, Middlesex and Essex and £24,000 for distribution to his children. Tom and John were to receive £10,000 each, Arthur and William £8,000 each and the three surviving sisters £10,000 each. To contribute towards payment of the debt John had persuaded his mother to take out a life insurance of £8000 for which she paid a premium of £571 per annum from 1808 to her death in 1824.[101]

Mary also transferred £37,000 worth of bank bonds, Consols and various other funds to the joint names of her sons, Joseph, Thomas and John. The transfer was upon trust to raise the sum of £5,000 by sale of the bonds within twelve months of her request or death and to purchase lands and property near to Hale.[102]

Whilst handling his own financial problems John continued to advise Robert Southey. Southey set out his anticipated income, expenditure and general affairs in some detail in May, asking for £50 to tide him over. The loan was repaid on 16th December of the same year.[103] The family friendship with the Coleridges continued as did John's help to 'The Colonel' James.

In September Joseph and his wife travelled to Ottery to see Maria and in December John offered to have John and Henry Coleridge to stay but George had already arranged alternative accommodation.[104]

There was a flurry of letters when Napoleon invaded Portugal. During the last quarter of 1807 the British started to leave the country and return home. Southey told his great friend Miss Barker: "My uncle and Harry were to take flight from Lisbon on the 12th of this month; they will probably come in a Liverpool ship, as they talk of seeing me soon, - but this is only a guess. If my uncle could get a passage in a King's ship, as one of his servants, he meant to prefer it".[105] In December he told John Rickman: "My uncle is arrived after a six weeks' passage."[106] Aunt Margaret noted her diary against 29th November, 1807: "Mr Coppendale arrived at Hale from Lisbon after 42 day's voyage - My Sister much agitated by his arrival, between joy at seeing him & sorrow that he was obliged to leave Portugal on account of the French Army advancing to take possession of it."[107]

The impending and actual invasion of Portugal had a further dramatic effect on the May family fortunes. This is clearly illustrated in Robert Southey's letters at the time.

In December he professed a hope that profits from his works may be used towards liquidating his debt to him and continued: "I am very anxious to hear how you have fared in this general wreck at Lisbon; and have some hope that as British property was not seized, your loss may have been lighter than you apprehended. I must look to you also for news of my Lisbon friends; and from my uncle I have only had one hurried letter, and Harry has not written a word to me since his return."[108]

He wrote again the next day: "Little did I suspect, my dear friend, when writing to you last night, what intelligence I should receive respecting you this evening . . . Absolute want, the want of the necessaries of life, is indeed of all evils the greatest; but, when decent comforts are left, how much better can all beyond these be spared than health, or friend, or child? To you, I trust, this is but a transient and recoverable loss . . . Assuredly no man ever employed wealth better; and I have something like a faith, that one who has employed it so well, will be entrusted with it again.

"My debt to you shall certainly be discharged in the course of the ensuing year. I explained the state of my affairs in my yesterday's letter . . .

"Should the Prince remove to Brazil, you will, I hope, consider and reconsider the matter well before you resolve upon removing to that country. I do not say that merely from personal feelings, and the pain which it would give me to have you at such a distance; but the stability of his government, in case of such an event, is to be doubted. Perhaps I may see you ere long . . . Should you be at Hale, that will be motive enough to lead me there."[109]

He informed C.W.Williams Wynn, Esq. M.P. on 19th December: "My uncle loses 300*l* a year by this expulsion of the English. My friend, John May, 20,000*l* (over £1,000,000). He is one of the best men I have ever known: it was not possible to make a better use of affluence than he did, or to part with it with more composure." He told Miss Barker on 21st December, 1807: "This expulsion of the English from Lisbon strips my uncle of half his income, - that half on which he himself lived; Miss Tyler and what he allowed Harry engrossing the other. My friend John May loses the bulk of his fortune by it - 20,000*l*. I know no man who ever made a better use of affluence, and there is none who will bear up against adversity more like a man. Whether my uncle's "great friends" will do anything for him remains to be seen. I generally suspect that a man's great friends are so called by the old law of contrarieties because they are very little his friends.[110]

Napoleon occupied Portugal in 1808. Many British returned home, but a number joined the Portuguese Court when it moved to Brazil. Southey's letters suggest that John considered joining them. His young family probably swayed him against it. His partner Mr Worthington returned to England on 10th April and frequently met the other partners, Mr Coppendale and William May, at Aunt Margaret's house for dinner. By August, however, William and Mr Worthington had sailed to Rio de Janeiro to open a house of business.[111] A committee of British merchants met in October in Rio de Janeiro to establish trading regulations, and to request Lord Srangford, the British Envoy, to arrange a place for a church and burial ground for the British community. One of the subscribing firms was that of Coppendale, May and Worthington. Meanwhile John kept his business connections in Lisbon. Southey journeyed to London and Hale where he met John, his wife and children. He wrote thanking them in June remembering the strong beer for which he had developed a taste. Whilst he encouraged John in his Brazil venture he argued that he should remain in England.[112&113]

The May family again visited Hale in the summer months sailing to the Isle of Wight for a fortnight. John travelled to Ottery on 10th September to visit the Coleridges and arrange for Johnny's future education at King's School. He met George and 'The Colonel' and probably Dr Warren the prospective headmaster.[114] Colonel James wrote to John at Hale three days later asking for his help and giving a fuller account of why, following General Simcoe's death and the loss of his staff position, he now only received the pay of a captain although he was a lieutenant colonel.[115]

1809 saw the commencement of young Johnny's education. He left home to start school at the age of seven. His Uncle Joseph wrote a letter of consolation to his brother John in May: "By a letter received yesterday from my mother I find your little John has quitted your roof for that of Miss Browde. This is an epoch in his life, & I cannot let it pass without expressing to you & to dear Susan a sincere & fervent wish that he may grow in health & strength in his new habitation, & that he may improve his mind as well as bodily frame, & that he may, in every respect fulfil the hopes you naturally entertain of him.

"Both Fanny & I do entirely enter into poor Susan's feelings on this occasion, we know from experience how painful it is, more especially for a mother, to part for the first time from her child; but the thing is now

'The Wick', Richmond Hill After a watercolour by J.J. Richards. C.1800.

over, and although Susan feels acutely she has, I trust, sufficient fortitude to support her under her latest trial however severe it may prove to her. I will not however dwell any longer on the subject; God bless the dear boy and may he . . . in all Seasons prove a comfort to his deserving Parents."[116]

John continued his business activities, giving insurance advice to Robert Southey regarding a £1000 life policy whilst Southey told John that he had long thought of writing to him concerning his "worldly affairs."[117] In August, 1810 Southey made a first ever repayment of £100 towards his 'indebtidness' to John.[118] Southey also asked John to obtain some books and information for him from his brother William in Brazil. John continued to stay with his Aunt at 4 Tavistock Street, Bedford Square, on Tuesdays or Wednesdays when he worked in London.[119]

The turn of 1809 to 1810 signalled a change in the property fortunes of the May and Southey families. Mr Buckmaster, Aunt Margaret's landlord, gave her notice to quit Tavistock Street in June but her sister Mary purchased the lease on 26th April, 1810.[120] John moved his family from Old Marsh to The Wick, Richmond Hill. The Wick had been built by the Scottish architect Robert Mylne in 1775 for Lady St Aubyn..It still stands at the top of Richmond Hill next door to Wick House, previously the home of Sir Joshua Reynolds. The Wick was at that time held on lease and it seems likely that John released some capital by the move. The house has two magnificent oval rooms overlooking the Thames. One of these rooms was John's study and library. It was favourably commented upon both by Samuel Taylor Coleridge in his visit of April, 1811, and Robert Southey in a letter of June, 1821.[121] The house has enjoyed a succession of famous occupants, more recently from the acting and music professions. Hale Manor remained in the ownership of John's mother.

Robert Southey had also been negotiating with his landlord regarding Greta Hall. In July he was able to inform his nephew that a new lease had been signed and that he had an option to stay for seven to fourteen years. Furthermore he had extended the size of his occupation.

Samuel Taylor Coleridge left Grasmere in May, 1810, to spend a few months at Greta Hall. By October he had decided to go to Edinburgh and place himself under treatment for his opium addiction with constant supervision from a medical practitioner. Basil Montagu, visiting William Wordsworth at the time, invited Samuel to accompany him to London, stay in his house and consult his friend and physician, Anthony Carlisle. Coleridge agreed to this plan but Wordsworth fearing that the arrangement would end in "mutual dissatisfaction" told Montagu the full extent of Coleridge's habits and the two agreed that it would be better for Samuel to stay at lodgings rather than in Montagu's house.

This discussion was kept from Samuel until his arrival in London when Basil Montagu told him that Wordsworth had "commissioned him to say, first, that he has no Hope of you; that for years past [you] had been an ABSOLUTE NUISANCE in the family; and that you were 'in the habit' of running into debt at a little Pot House for Gin." Likewise, William Wordsworth was reported to have spoken of Samuel Taylor Coleridge as a "rotten drunkard" who was "rotting out his entrails by intemperance".[122] Samuel, devastated by his friend's disclosures, crept off to Hudson's Hotel in Covent Garden.

The situation deteriorated even further when Anthony Carlisle, who had been approached in a professional capacity, spoke openly of Coleridge's opium habit "to a Woman, who made it the subject of common Table Talk". Coleridge and Wordsworth did not speak or communicate for the next year and a half but the two families and mutual friends discussed the matter. Wordsworth bitterly resented the inference that he was to blame for Coleridge's sufferings. Coleridge for his part

Old School House, Ottery.

continued to blame Wordsworth. The falling out continued for two years until a kind of reconciliation was accomplished in May, 1812, aided by John May.

"Little Johnny" was accompanied by his parents to Ottery "to Mr Coleridge's School" on Monday 20th August, 1810, wrote Aunt Margaret. On 30th John and Susan returned accompanying "Master Coleridge". At the end of his first term Johnny travelled to Hale and stayed for a week before leaving for Richmond with his father on Christmas day.[123] In January, 1811, George Coleridge asked the parents for a report on how they thought Johnny was progressing after his first term: "I expect to hear from you soon, when I must desire you will be explicit as to your opinion of your little Boy. You must hide nothing from me thro' delicacy if you wish any alteration: as I am assured you will give me full and more than full praise, if I deserve any."[124]

Having had a chance to observe Johnny on his return to school after the holidays, George made a further report at the end of February. He was pleased with his progress and thought that his holiday had been of benefit to him, "I really think him improved by having been home - for he is more steady than when he left us before Xmas and performs more lessons and in a better manner than he used so that I begin to have a respect for his faculty of memory. He has likewise a good character at the Schoolhouse for attending to what is enjoined on him." He seems to have had the normal exuberance of a nine year old boy as George reported: "the loco-motive faculty will not easily bear restraint after school, particularly when his eye seemed quite well and we could find no excuse for confinement." At the time Johnny was suffering from an inflammation of his eye and the school was treating it with his grandmother's special recipe.[125]

Johnny made friends with John Awdry and the two soon got into trouble at school. Fair Day at Ottery was approaching and the lads concocted a scheme to get themselves more money to spend at the fair. George had to give John another report on his son's behaviour: "The state of the case, as far as I can learn from your Son, is simply this - understanding that the Ottery Fair was to be held during the next week and that they would not be allowed as much money as they wished to spend, they agreed that a snug seven shilling piece each would be a pretty addition and that their moneyholders would know nothing of the matter. They therefore determined to apply to Mr Copendale, who, they presumed from his late liberality, would easily supply them with what they wanted. This, I believe, is a pretty correct paraphrase of Johnny May's short account to me - viz - that they wanted the money for the Fair. The plan, I presume, came from J Awdry, who has his money stopt at the Colonel's by my desire, until he confirms more strictly to school discipline. When proposed to J. May, self-interest, I conceive, made him acquiesce without any further consideration on the subject than the greater opportunity he should have of seeing Shows and buying Toys, etc on the Fair day." Having Johnny with him as he finished his letter he added a postscript: "He says that J Awdry told him he'd want some money for the Fair and whether he should get any for him from Mr Copendale to wch J May replied, he should like five shillings. J Awdry proposed half a guinea each but as John May adhered to five shillings, they thought it best to split the difference."

As well as getting up to normal schoolboy pranks Johnny enjoyed gardening in the school grounds with Mrs George Coleridge. His eyes continued to suffer, an ailment he shared with his father. "The Boys are making little Gardens in the School Courtyard and I understand that John would not be an idle spectator and so meddled with the earth, wch could not have been beneficial to his eye but probably injurious."[127]

In April Johnny was taken ill with typhus. He was nursed by George Coleridge's wife. When scarlet fever struck the school, he was moved to the care of Mrs Luke Coleridge. In May, George Coleridge was concerned enough to write to his father suggesting that little Johnny had better be moved to Hale directly. Unfortunately his condition worsened to such an extent that George and Mrs Luke Coleridge thought he should not travel. They arranged for a Honiton physician to care for him. He reported that, "From the natural perspiration, the calmness of his patient, and the state of his pulse, he has every reason to hope that nothing serious can happen".[128] John travelled to see his son towards the end of May. Until his illness Johnny's education had proceeded well and George Coleridge reported: "I should tell you that John has worked thro' his Syntax manfully twice and is now going thro' it a third time. Then we shall practice him in every part of grammar and class him."[129]

Samuel Taylor Coleridge having severed relationships with all his family left his wife, Sara, to bring up their children at Greta Hall, Keswick, with her sister, Edith, and brother-in-law, Robert Southey. He moved to Hammersmith. John May invited Samuel's two nephews, John Taylor and Henry Nelson, to stay at The Wick for a while in April, 1811. The boys were busy with studies in their vacation and accepted the invitation "in part" staying one week.[130] The invitation had been made with George Coleridge's full knowledge and agreement and with the intention of facilitating a reconciliation between Samuel and the boys. He thanked him for his kindness in arranging the forthcoming visit.[131] The visit was a great success and John Taylor thanked May: "I never spent so many days of such real happiness at once in my life and I shall prove this by accepting your general invitation whenever it is in my power."[132] A similar weekend invitation was made to Samuel at Hammersmith that he readily accepted, visiting Richmond on 20th and 21st April. He slept at a local inn, but took all his meals at The Wick.

John Taylor Coleridge was becoming close friends with John, who advanced him several loans of money to follow his career at the Bar, go travelling and assist his marriage plans. Later he also became a mentor to Johnny. John Taylor recorded his impressions of the April meeting at Richmond both in a letter home to his brother James and later to brother Henry, that he, in turn, incorporated in 'Specimens of the Table Talk of the late Samuel Taylor Coleridge'. The earlier letter recounts, "When I saw my Uncle Sam last in town I gave him a copy" (of his successful

Latin verse) "by his own desire, and he promised to write me by the next penny post. I need hardly say that I have not heard one word from him! Every subject he was master of, and discussed in the most splendid eloquence, without pausing for a word. Whether poetry, religion, language, politics, or metaphysics were on the 'tapis', he was equally at home and equally clear. It was curious to see the ladies loitering most attentively, and being really uncommonly entertained with a long discussion of two hours on the deepest metaphysics. At the end of this time I got one of them, a beautiful woman, and a superior singer, to sing some Italian Aria to him. His very frame shook with pleasure, a settled smile and a sort of tittering noise indicated his feelings. He prayed that she might finish those strains in Heaven, and, sitting down by Mrs May, recited some extempore verses on the singer.

"When he saw us first he was affected distressingly, and through the whole time he was affectionate in the highest degree. Henry" (Henry Nelson) "delights him beyond measure. He made a conquest of all the men and women at Richmond, gave us analyses of long works which are to come out, recited songs and odes of his own, told stories of his youth and travels, never sparing himself at all, and altogether made the most powerful impression on my mind of any man I ever saw.

"Yet I saw and heard some things which I did not quite like."[133]

The later recollections written for Henry add that on 21st April before breakfast, Coleridge was found by his nephew in "Mr May's delightful book-room, where he was in silent admiration of the prospect." Later in the day he sat down by Professor Rigaud with whom he entered into a discussion of Kant's System of Metaphysics.[134] Over the weekend the four men walked to the Royal Observatory at Richmond where they again met with Professor Rigaud. Samuel Taylor Coleridge was particularly intrigued by the model of an arch constructed by Atwood and subsequently asked John: "If possible, you would procure for me, or inform me where I can myself procure, any distinct account or engraving of the model"[135]

The same year John threw his house and garden open again in another attempt to facilitate a healing of relationships, this time between Samuel Taylor Coleridge and William Wordsworth. Robert Southey stayed in London from June and towards the end of July, he and his wife walked with Samuel in the peace of The Wick garden. Samuel told the Southeys the full story of the estrangement from his point of view. He wrote to Wordsworth in May, 1812: "It became my Duty to state the whole affair to them, even as the means of transmitting it to you."[136]

Susan May was expecting once more and in August James Coleridge sent his best wishes for her health and his thanks for looking after his daughter Fanny. Charlotte Livius May was born on 16th September and baptised in Richmond on 14th November.

As George Coleridge and his wife grew older so Mr and Mrs Warren took on more responsibility. James Coleridge mentioned that Mrs Warren made "a most excellent Mistress of a School, her fellow would not have been found; for activity; tenderness and liberality: I think we all gainers by the alteration."[137] By the start of October George had decided to retire as headmaster "on Christmas night". His reasons were more than age and involved spending more time educating his son with an eye to the church. His motives, he told John, "are many and must be left for discussion until I have the pleasure of seeing you."[138] The same month John and Frances Duke Coleridge (Fanny) stayed at Hale on their way to Ottery where John remained a few days with his old tutor and friend supporting him and discussing the forthcoming retirement plans.

George Coleridge finally retired in December 1811 and wrote a long letter to his friend expressing his feelings and describing the occasion. "On Monday last between the hours of ten and twelve a.m. I left my school for the last time as its Master amid the affectionate tears of my Boys. - At half past ten having arranged all preliminaries for the ensuing Holidays, I set myself in order to address them for the last time but the thoughts, I think, of the time when I finish quickened that school for Oxford with the multitude of unexpected and undeserved blessings that I had since received with the affectionate honours intended me by the Children so filled my heart, that I was for some time speechless. A few tears however relieved me, and I was enabled with some few interruptions to give an account of my retiring, to recommend my successor, to appreciate fairly the kindness of my dear Boys and with as much grace as my feelings would permit ... Shortly after I was waited on by five or six of the head Boys bearing their present, which uncommonly handsome and beautiful as it is, would have had no value in my estimation, if it had not been beset by the most valuable of all ornaments, the love of my Boys, and the affectionate zeal of yourself and my Brother."[139]

John May asked Robert Southey to write an inscription for a gift he intended to present to George on his retirement. Southey turned his friend down firstly on account of his not having written Latin for seventeen years and secondly due to time constraints: "You see, therefore, that I have no chance of having verse of mine engraved on silver. If I could do it to my own satisfaction I would most cheerfully, though there are two poets in the family, by either of whom an inscription might be supplied. I certainly think, considering the relation in which the donors stand to G. Coleridge, that the inscription should be in Latin. The thing should be classical."[140]

John Taylor Coleridge had already sent John his ideas for an inscription adding that they should be rejected if Southey sent any verses.[141] It was his inscription that graced John's gift to George who was very moved. "The praise which the bearing, eloquence and affection of my Nephew John has penned and with my dearest and best Friend has thought fit to appropriate to me, ought not to be disfigured by subsequent blemishes."[142]

Some authorities suggest that George Coleridge retired in 1808. Contemporary correspondence and facts already outlined above throw some doubt on that conclusion.

The retirement of George Coleridge precipitated a move of school for young Johnny. George told his parents he was satisfied with all their arrangements regarding Johnny apart from the school's vicinity. He counselled the parents that the effect of the location must be countered by their determination to ensure that he be kept strictly under school discipline.[143] George, as his schoolmaster, had recognised a rebellious streak in Johnny's character. In February John Taylor advised John regarding the merits of Charles Burney and his private school at Greenwich. It had a good reputation with regard to the health, care and comfort of up to one hundred boys aged fourteen to fifteen. The situation was good and the cost about one hundred pounds per annum. "I wish you could meet Burney as I am sure you would be pleased with him."[144]

Charles Burney was a famous bibliophile and Greek scholar. He ran his school until 1813, resigning in favour of his son Rev. Charles Parr Burney. He died in 1817 and his library was purchased by the British Museum. It is ironic in the light of future events in Johnny's life that a rebellion amongst the pupils at Burney's school in 1808 is chronicled in a letter home written by John Graham a pupil at the time.[145]

George referred again to Johnny's character in October, 1812, when he told John that it gave him great pleasure to hear that Johnny was making progress in his learning but warned: "This pleasing circumstance will not I trust prevent you from removing him from Richmond." He added that he felt Johnny should not only be removed from Richmond but from any place close to it. He told John that his son had good talents but needed a "temperate yet a determined master"[146] who would keep his nose to the grindstone.

Robert Southey now wrote to John pointing out an article that he had written in The Quarterly concerning a certain Dr Bell.[147] Dr Bell was born on 27th March, 1753, in the City of St Andrews the son of Alexander & Margaret Bell. He sailed for India on 21st February, 1787, where, declining salary or payment, he superintended the Military Male Orphan Asylum at Madras run on his 'Madras' system of education. In 1797 he landed again at Portsmouth and set about introducing his 'Madras system' to Great Britain, at first to St Bartolph's in 1798, then to Kendal schools in 1799 followed by Keswick and Grasmere in the Lake District. George Coleridge introduced the system to the Ottery parish school in 1813.[148] Southey was a strong supporter of Dr Bell and became his biographer.[149]

Fate would dictate that the Mays on their Tour to the Lakes in 1822, should share the same coach as Dr Bell, whilst travelling from Rydal to Keswick and then spend many evenings of discussion together whilst staying at Greta Hall during the following three weeks.

Throughout 1811, whilst helping his friends, John May was worried about the situation in Brazil and in particular the conduct and safety of his brother William. 1812 started badly with an unpaid debt and progressively worsened. The family waited anxiously to hear from William and also for the arrival of a bullion shipment. By August George Coleridge expressed concern regarding the material outlook for John and his family as well as for his mental health. He advised John to look at his situation at its worst and to try to find a way to disentangle himself and his partners from their venture in Brazil. "The best advice I can give you next to this, is to look your situation full in its face, to meet it in its most grisly form, that you may be able rationally to find some expedient for disentanglement. You will not, I am afraid, engage in another speculation until you either are, or have well grounded hopes that you shall be freed in a limited time from the one that now embarrasses you: for you must do nothing that eventually may make you repent of your own persistency and add a sting to unavoidable misfortune. It is very probable that your pressing letters, and a sense of the serious calamity which has been brought on you may quicken your partners in the settlement of transatlantic concerns and put you in possession of your real state before the absolute expiration of the Partnership. In this case, you may safely embark afresh in the speculation, which you have in view."[150]

Regarding John's future prospects he commented: "Should it however please God that you should not move in so elevated a line of life, your sphere of beneficence only will be circumscribed, but not your happiness." Johnny was also giving John problems as George observed "Your account of Johnny's minute improvement does not much surprise me. To have abilities and to use these abilities conscientiously and industriously are quite different things in all conditions of life: but the difference is more observable and probably more consequential in that of a School Master than in any other.

John again had plans to go to Rio de Janeiro which worried his friends including Robert Southey who told him: "The loss of property may be repaired, & the success of one year make amends for the reverses of another, but time past in a foreign country away from out nearest and dearest ties, is an irretrievable loss of comfort & happiness."[151] Only two weeks earlier he had felt able to ask John to acquire a set of Muratori's great collection of the Italian Historians from High Holborn.[152]

As the situation deteriorated William returned to England on October 23rd, stayed one day at Hale before going to London to see John May and Mr Coppendale and then returned to Brazil on 7th December.[153] John still planned to end his Brazilian venture and George reassured him that at least following his brother's visit he could now see his enemy face to face and that his situation should be retrievable with help from his true friends. John Taylor Coleridge praised him for his Christian conduct in his trials and continued "I hope you found William still impressed as you left him with a sense of his own failings and an anxious determination to make all the amends in his power, something I should hope might be done in diminution of your losses during the remainder of your connection with America."[154] William's visit home somehow settled John's anxieties and uncertainties regarding the future of the Brazilian branch of his ventures. Following the collapse of his interests there he decided to make a break from the country which he did, as George put it, "unhurt in conscience or honor"[155]

John May proceeded next with the 'speculation' alluded to by George. He went into partnership with an established business of wine merchants of the Stert family and the new firm had the name Stert and May. Throughout his negotiations he consulted George Coleridge who was only too pleased to offer advice, encouragement and help. "It would be presumption in me to give my opinion of the line of business in which you are embarked. I rely on your prudence and knowledge of mercantile matters that it is a wise step, wch you have taken. My business is to be aidant and assistant in its success and that I will be to the utmost stretch of my powers and influence, ever searching how limited my services to you ever have been and how limited they are still likely to be. You yield up the easy duties of Friendship to your Friends and retain the difficult ones to yourself. You are prepared to make any sacrifices for those you love, while you content yourself with the reflection that your friends are prepared to do the same for you. This is indeed the true test of friendship and yourself a living example of its truth. But I ought to hasten to tell you that your Friends at Heath's Court as well as at the Warden House are rejoiced at the arrangement well you have made for your future temporal welfare, and have set themselves in right earnest (as we say in Devon) to further your success and to extend the name of Stert and May beneficially. It will be necessary however that we should be able to give an answer to questioners. It will be asked by many who cannot exactly enter into our feelings, what wines of different kinds can be rendered [from] your house or the Exeter quay including car carriage and insurance. Whether there is any deduction (as is the case at Granger's) to those who pay ready money, and whatever other particulars may suggest themselves to you as necessary to be answered to those who are undertaking the important business of stocking their cellars. For the success of our endeavors we cannot be answerable, for the strenuous and active exertion we can and ought to be answerable and I am not without hopes that the effect will tally with the cause.

"It is indeed a fortunate circumstance that you could get into an established firm on such advantageous terms, terms wch it may be said, have been procured by your own character for probable intelligence and industry that you should have connected yourself with a Person, who can be as far as possible from disguising the real state of his affairs, and that your connection will lie among people with whom you have been in the habit of doing business for so many years. It is fortunate too that you are permitted to reside at Richmond a circumstance wch will conduce at the same time to your health your comfort and probably your interest."[156]

Through 1813 John also maintained his insurance and finance businesses, discussing a premium with Southey in January and advising on an investment in August.[157] His main mercantile concerns however faced debts of some £45,000, equivalent to over two million pounds today. The principal debtor, Mr Charles Brandling, an M.P with estates in Yorkshire, appears to have strung the business along from February, 1813, until May, 1816, promising to liquidate his Yorkshire assets. Joseph apparently lacked the will to enforce payment whist telling John that he would wish to find him £10,000 which he "needs in his present difficulties". Mary May's spending at Hale Manor was also becoming a real problem to her family.[158]

Matters got so bad that Joseph eventually had to leave his house in Bramshaw to move into Hale Manor with his mother and John seriously considered moving from The Wick. He was temporarily cheered up by a visit from Southey in the autumn of 1813.[159] The move continued to be very much a possibility in January of 1815 and Southey wrote: "I well know how much it must cost you to leave so delightful a habitation as that at Richmond."[160] Through March and June he enquired again but John weathered the storm and remained at The Wick for the time being.

Johnny was put down for Eton and moved schools in the spring of 1813. This move was probably partly preparatory to Eton and partly to comply with George Coleridge's advice the previous year.

A further calamity overtook his father when he lost the largely uninsured cargo of a captured Express Packet. William had reached Brazil again in the spring and John looked forward to the final ending of his foreign partnership by August. In December George offered to help John both financially by advancing him a sum of money for three years and in education by taking Johnny on as a private tutor, providing him with board and lodging and assisting him to go to Mr Warren's school. "I entreat you to make use of this Sum, and as soon as I get your answer of consent, I will give orders for its being sold out for your use, or transferred into whosoever name you please. Your success, I know, depends on the preservation of your credit, and that cannot be preserved by answering all legal demands. If you are not able to do this thro' unforeseen accidents or the villainy of mankind, which no prudence could have counteracted, it is your duty to call for help on those friends, whom you would in similar circumstances have relieved if you had had the power. I myself should have looked to you alone, if I had been encompassed with difficulty and it is but just that you should take what advantage you can of my little means to aid in extricating yourself from a situation into which you have fallen without any fault of your own. And thus much for your public concerns which naturally lead to the consideration of your domestic.

"You may think that you cannot well be too lavish in paying for the Education of your Son, and therefore intend to fix him where he will receive sound instruction and elegant breeding at the same time. But this should not be done but in cases of superfluity nor according to my mind scarcely in any case for the luxury of education almost ever interferes with the perceptive part of it, and sends forth into public a sensualist instead of a Scholar. I do not, my dearest Friend, offer my services wch are now nearly effete, for any presumption, that I am capable of superintending the education of your Son as well as the Person to whom you intended to commit him but if the expenses of that School be great (as I suspect they are) to which you are about to send him, I think the present aspect of your affairs might induce you and Mrs May to think of an arrangement at Ottery, which for your sake I will cheerfully take on myself. Mr Warren's school is now proceeding on a good plan and he will after the Xmas Holidays have the advantage of an assistant strongly recommended to him by Provost of Oriel. The Writing Master is likewise a clever and industrious young man and there is a good French Master who attends the School. John will board and lodge at my house, and have me as his private Tutor and your Godson now at the head of the School, as his Protector. The [   ] plan, I am aware was unpleasing to Mrs May, but [   ] seeing that John may have attained to firmer health and that circumstances call on you to retrench every superfluous expense, I could not think that I had entirely fulfilled the duty of a Friend, if I had omitted suggesting it to your considerations."[161]

The very generous offer was not taken up.

The Colonel, James Coleridge, visited John in 1813 and described the journey home: "Coming home on ye arrival of ye coach no inside places could be found and we mounted outside. Excepting some hard rain for an hour over Bagshot our Journey was very delightful."[162]

Robert Southey was appointed Poet Laureate from 12th August and enjoyed a social whirl in London dining with John May and the Coleridges amongst many others. He asked John to obtain a letter of Attorney empowering him to receive all monies payable to him as Poet Laureate.[163]

John May now frequently met John Taylor Coleridge in London and told his father in 1814 how the more he met him the more he and all his family held him in warm affection and esteem.[164] In June John offered him a loan by way of a letter of credit on Paris. It was accepted at £100, less than the figure offered, the principal to be repaid in five years.[165]

The winter of 1814 was extremely cold and John Taylor with all the May family crossed the frozen Thames on foot on 23rd January. The ice, although smooth enough for skaters in places, was mostly piled up in large masses.[166]

John's financial situation in 1814 is somewhat confusing and possibly indicative of a careless philanthropic side of his nature towards friends. From the summer of 1813 an affair at the London Assurance Office had begun to go wrong. He could not obtain money from Brazil, was owed a considerable sum in debts and had strong thoughts of moving from The Wick. Nevertheless he financed a foreign tour for John Taylor Coleridge advancing a further £300 when the first money ran out. He considered that a prolongation of the tour would be "economically laid out in the perfection of those mental powers with which God has blessed him." Distressing financial circumstances precluded John's largesse being repeated for his own son a few years later, although he had arranged to send him to Eton. Furthermore John advanced £50 to Southey in July of that year.[167] As late as November, his brother Joseph wrote to him, in reply to a letter to his mother regarding his future manner of living, sympathising with him regarding the continuing possibility of his having to leave The Wick. He expressed concern at the effect this might have upon his health: "For the unwelcome prospect you hold forth of leaving that residence which is endeared to you by such a variety of considerations; it is in truth my dear John a great sacrifice that you are making, I know it from the feelings that I experience at this present moment, . . . the only fear I have in your case is the diminution of that good health which the pure air of Richmond has now for so many years heaped you with."[168]

George also wrote to John in November having heard of new business plans following the end of his Brazilian ventures in which he had lost a fortune largely due to his brother William's negligence. His entrepreneurial instincts were leading him towards another venture and George Coleridge wrote a supportive letter to his old pupil whilst pointing out the continuing financial assistance being given by Uncle Coppendale: "It is a melancholy sort of satisfaction yet it is a satisfaction, after such a sea of troubles, losses and anxieties to have found at length the end of your Brazilian concerns.

"There are many Truths and determinations of conduct to which we instantly give our assent. The mind refuses to wade thro' a syllogism, the conclusion of which, is seen as if intuitively. Of such a nature is the reasonableness of the plan, which you have detailed to me for your future arrangement: and it is such a one, as I should long since have been forward to have suggested to you, had you not assigned so much importance to the matter of an undiminished establishment as necessary for your credit. That your determination is correctly right, is to a mind constituted as yours is, a sufficient reason, why eventually it should be pleasing. The apparent change is very reconcilable without the least diminution of your credit. That the state of your business should require your constant residence in Town, I should reason, is a proof rather of its augmentation than its diminution and must, it should seem, be a fair answer to the inquisitive and prying public. But if I should see in this mode of reasoning the determination is still honorable and should therefore be adopted. My concern is chiefly about the health of yourself Mrs May and your Family."[169]

Uncertainty over his occupation of The Wick remained until March, 1815. John remained actively involved in financial affairs managing £2,056 of investments in Navy 5% Annuities for Mr James Gwilliam and Elizabeth Best both of Richmond, in respect of their forthcoming marriage.[170]

George Coleridge supplied John with cider from time to time and in May sent a Hogshead to Stert & May's Wine Merchants and another to the "Cyder Factor" for them to forward it to Breamore. The Coleridge family were all supplied by John and in August James and Edward sent him a total of £138.14.0. in payment. George Coleridge's income at this time was £700 per annum.[171]

Samuel Taylor Coleridge was hitting a 'rock bottom' of Opium addiction and, in February, Southey expressed his feelings to John telling him that: "His utter neglect of his wife & children is becoming every day more serious."[172] When Joseph Cottle asked Southey for his help in setting up an annuity to aid Samuel's recovery he received short shrift and a reply in April referring to "Coleridge's most culpable habits of sloth and self-indulgence." He argued that an annuity should only be considered where the recipient "is disabled from exerting himself - or where his exertions are unproductive," but Coleridge was "in neither of these predicaments." Southey was wholly unsympathetic to Coleridge himself and not interested in the causes or reasons for addiction. He had had to deal with the consequences in the shape of the broken family that he had taken under his roof. He told Cottle: "Nothing is wanting to make him easy in circumstances and happy in himself, but to leave off opium and devote a certain portion of his time to the discharge of his duty."[173] He wrote to John in July telling him that he was writing to Samuel regarding his treatment of his family and that if he did not have a reply by the beginning of August he would have to assume that Samuel had deserted them in all respects. "If, as I expect, my letter be not answered, I shall write to you at length upon the subject."[174]

By September, having unsuccessfully given Samuel several ultimatums concerning the welfare of his children, he had to request help from both John May[175] and, through him, Colonel James Coleridge[176] to finance a place for Hartley Coleridge at Merton College, Oxford. To John he wrote, "The father [Samuel] must be considered as a man labouring under a kind of moral madness." He was careful to emphasise that he had only expressed his opinions to Wordsworth and John himself. George Coleridge corresponded with John regarding the request for Hartley's place and in September asked him to convey the Coleridge family's offer to assist Sam's family "help the Wheel out of the Rut" with their thanks to Mr Southey.[177] Colonel James also wrote: "Southey seems to have behaved most kindly and generously whilst their Mad father is at Bristol, or God knows where, living on the bounty of his friends. I expect that that Stream will dry up and then we must have a heavier blow unless Opium or something removed him to another World. What a humbling lesson to all men is Samuel Coleridge."

Robert Southey writing in January, 1815, after sympathising with John over the likely loss of The Wick, commented on the success of his arrangements for Hartley going up to Oxford saying, "This is a great thing accomplished." Regarding Hartley he felt that if he did not now make his own way in the world it would be his own fault as up to now there was no sign that he would pay for the "sins of his father". He had heard nothing of Samuel and expected that he was doing nothing. "Sooner or later this must lead to the most deplorable consequences - for tho by mere accident (as it may almost be called) his family are preserved from absolute want, & his children from ruin, I know not what is ultimately to keep him from a prison."

Later in the year he observed that Hartley was "in many respects ominously like his father" and "He has a disposition to justify whatever he does".[178] The themes of "lack of will power" and "justifying" were ones he returned to repeatedly over the years. In December, 1818, whilst sympathising with John over a major family tragedy he found time to comment regarding Hartley: "About his future prospects I am by no means hopeful. There is far too much of his father in his disposition. . . . He has the same subtlety in finding reasons to justify his own habits & inclinations."[179] In May, 1819, after commenting regarding Hartley Coleridge's success at Oriel, he continued: "It remains to be seen what life he will make of his great talents. I am afraid he has too much of his father's subtlety of mind & too little of its compass."[180]

William May returned to England from Brazil in October, 1814, and John was at last rid of a venture which had cost him much money as well as heartache. Over the performance of his brother George commended John for setting William back on the road to recovery in the world especially as he had been the cause of so many of his misfortunes and concluded: "I trust that he will by that future and well doing live to make you some amends for the thousand anxieties which you have suffered by his means. Experience is often the only Teacher - and to him I believe it has been a rigid one. Time alone will show what effect its lessons have had. I most truly wish him success."[181]

In the autumn of 1815 Southey travelled to view the battlefield of Waterloo. He wrote his poem *The Poet's Pilgrimage to Waterloo* and dedicated it to his friend. The inscription reads: "To John May, after a friendship of twenty years, this poem is inscribed in testimony of the highest esteem and affection, by Robert Southey." The poem was published in 1816.[182]

Johnny May signed the Entrance Book at Eton College on 17th September, 1815, "Aged 13, Born March 8".[183] He is stated to be in Remove in the College List for 1815. At about the same time there is a record of 'Colonel' James noting the travel cost in December, 1816 for

> TO
>
> # JOHN MAY,
>
> AFTER A FRIENDSHIP OF TWENTY YEARS,
>
> THIS POEM IS INSCRIBED
>
> IN TESTIMONY OF THE HIGHEST ESTEEM AND
> AFFECTION,
>
> BY
>
> ROBERT SOUTHEY.

Dedication to John May in 'The Poet's Pilgrimage to Waterloo' 1816.

the 140 miles from Eton to Honiton: "For a Post-Chaise carrying two people at 1s. 3d. per mile - £8. 15s. By Coach outside, £2. 5s. or inside, £3. 15s .12".[184]

George Coleridge, as always, was the first to write a letter of congratulations to John. On 22nd September he says he was glad that John May and his own nephew, John Taylor, now considered that Johnny's education was advanced enough in the classics to ensure that he could yet take full advantage of the opportunities offered in Eton where if "the elements have been well learned" there is room for "able Masters to teach". He hoped that Johnny would now repay John for "your anxiety, trouble and expense by his good behaviour and solid progress in

Dr Keate's Eton College Register - September 1815.
By Courtesy of the Provost and Fellows of Eton College.

useful learning". He suggested that John confine himself to wishes regarding Johnny's future rather than hopes as he said, "Excessive hope can scarcely ever be realized and the disappointment of hope is so leaden a concern as a Child is calippered by feelings from within and from without. I enjoin this advice on you from the observation which I have made in the case of four out of six of the excellent Fathers that I have known and I strive daily to impress the lesson firmly on my own Mind."[185]

Johnny's entrance must have been a shaft of sunlight in his father's life at a time when his finances continued to suffer throughout 1816 and 1817. His difficulties elicited comforting letters from the Coleridges and Southey who wanted to know: "By what principle, or what strange want of principle, is it that mercantile men so often, for the sake of the shortest reprieve from bankruptcy, involve their nearest friends and connections with them."[186] He also requested John to act as an executor of his will. This was agreed to. Following Edith's death on 16th November, 1837, and his subsequent marriage to Caroline Bowles, Southey changed his will and appointed different executors. In April, Southey lost his son and in his grief again contemplated moving to London close to John. By October he had changed his mind and his affairs were doing so well he was able to send John a draft "upon Longmans for 100*l*. at three day's sight."[187]

By 1817, Johnny had progressed to the Fifth Form - Lower Division. He seems to have lost touch with previous friends at Ottery as John's godson George May mentioned to him in February, "I hope you have good and satisfactory accounts of John from Eton. He is quite become a stranger to me, and we have not met since he left Ottery school."[188] Matters had remained fairly calm and John heard from Southey that he had not had to claim from the Equitable Insurance Office by his "venturing to sea uninsured."[189] Events were however shortly to take several turns for the worse in the lives of both John Mays.

John's favourite Aunt Margaret died at 4 Tavistock Street in January and he was executor of her will. Having made bequests of £3,000 each to her sisters, £3000 to her nephew, John, and a number of smaller bequests to friends and servants, she left the residue of her estate to him. Number 4, Tavistock Street, Bedford Square, thus passed to John May.

Johnny's character and general behaviour at Eton gave George Coleridge some considerable cause for concern and, in the autumn of 1817, he asked John for a report: "I wish to know too more in detail the state of Johnny's improvement" in his learning and attitude. He said, "I know how much his conduct may operate on your happiness."[190] The following January he asked John for another report after the Christmas holidays. Next June he wrote: "You will soon have Johnny with you, and I own that I should like to hear your report of him."[191] George, as an experienced schoolmaster, was increasingly concerned about Johnny and with good reason.

The headmaster of Eton College was John Keate. He had encountered opposition from the boys to his appointment in 1810 and this continued as he changed college rules concerning the imposition of a 5 o'clock absence. This may have been a catalyst for the Eton Rebellion of 1818. One source holds the Rebellion was prompted by Dr Keate's desire to stop the hunting, shooting, and tandem driving then in vogue among the boys.[192] A contemporary letter suggests that it did not begin from Keate's "wanting to catch fellows hunting, shooting and driving, but because they made a noise going up into five o'clock school on the Friday before".[193] The diary of Dr Keate's sister-in-law, Miss Margaretta

Brown, would seem to back up the first suggestion. She refers to hunting on 29th October, 29th writing: "Mr Keate has been so plagued lately with this audacious plan of the boys going out hunting early on a morning that I am quite angry with them." and by the 31st recorded that the boys had written "Floreat Etona" on the walls of the Long Walk and: "A great many boys were standing in the Long Walk, all of them very loud and riotous - I was much frightened at hearing a violent crash from the Greene's house."[194] The boys broke all the windows on the front of the house. Dr Keate wrote to parents in December, after the events, explaining that he had imposed the absence as a punishment for gross misconduct, but not till after the boys had been warned by him of his intention, "and had it in their power to avoid it by returning to a sense of their Duty."[195]

The situation erupted on Tuesday 3rd November. It is described in a letter, dated Tuesday 4th November, written by Edward John Stanley (2nd Baron Stanley) to his Sister Miss Louisa Stanley in Anglesea: "I have indeed been very lazy of late, but we had such disturbances, and so much to do, that I have not really been able to find time. Keate has thought fit to put a new absence at 5 o'clock, which naturally made a good deal of row, and was not particularly admired. A boy named Marriott was sent away for not going home when one of the Masters told him. The boy being very much liked, the next day when all the boys were assembled, one of them in a loud voice called out - 'Where's Marriott', followed by a volley of hisses and shouts; this drove the Doctor from his Elevation, but he was not allowed to descend in quiet, for, before he reached the Door about 4 or 5 eggs were thrown at him, tho' I believe very little touched him.

"After he had gone out and left us in the School, the work of demolition began; the forms, which are nailed to the floor, were broken up by a sledge hammer, and the pieces thrown about. Presently, after the Doctor returned, accompanied by all his satellites, viz., six of the Masters of the Upper School, with their assistance he was enabled to proceed for that time without further molestation. He threatened to expel publicly the first boy who after this should do anything which could possibly be laid hold of by the Masters to send him away. However, at five the next day all not choosing to retire quietly to their habitations, assembled near the road, they pulled down part of the wall, and broke a good many of the School windows; one of the Master's looking thro' the blinds of his house to mark who he should see throw a stone. One of the company, observing his situation, threw a stone at the window, and hit the very pane of glass he was looking out of, broke the blind and very near hit him on the head.

Things, however, were patched up in a way till this night, when the Doctor said he would expel a boy who he knew to have been in the crowd, though he had not been seen throwing; and likewise several others. This was considered as a breach of a kind of Agreement which had been made by the boys being quiet, and Keate saying that he hoped there would be no more disturbance, and that all was over; however, having threatened to expel this boy, this morning they went into the School, and with a crow and large hammer knocked down the Doctor's Throne. The unfortunate man when he arrived was extremely astonished at the disappearance of his accustomed seat, and ran about like one of the guinea pigs at the Poultry Yard. - A poor wretched little Colleger was caught coming out of School about the time this was done, he, being carried away triumphantly, was bullied, badgered and baited by all 10 Masters till they got a kind of confession of who was concerned in pulling about the Doctor's Desk down about his ears.

"After church to-day we all assembled in the School, and six boys were expelled publicly for being concerned in it. After they had marched, Keate was prosing, and said he hoped it would make the remainder more quiet, to which one of the Sixth Form said 'never' to himself, and was immediately publicly expelled. The Doctor threatens to send away a good many more who were in the Assembly, tho' they did not throw stones or destroy anything else. I have only just time to write this before the post."[196]

Margaretta Brown's diary for Tuesday 3rd November recounted the events from the 'Official' side when she wrote, "After breakfast Williams (came) in to say that Cartland has come over to say Mr Keate's desk has been entirely destroyed by some boys - there is no end to their audacity and folly. It really puts me quite in a fidget. Mr Keate went over at his usual time. He is always cool, and collected; but he must be much annoyed at all this. Mr Keate came home for a minute before church and told Fanny that six boys had been found out and would be expelled - two Collegers, Pitt and White, Oppidans, two Eltons, May and Jackson.

"The way the business of the desk was found was this - Cartland heard a great knocking in the Upper School - he went up and found Mr

Keate's desk was nearly demolished but all the boys had fled. He then recollected that half an hour before he had seen that idle pickle Lloyd in the Upper School who said he had been looking for a book. Upon hearing this Mr Keate sent for him and he and all the other Masters examined him for above two hours - For the first hour he told one lie after another, but he at last so entangled himself that he burst into tears and confirmed that although he had had no hand in the destruction of the desk that he knew of their intention to do so - having heard the two Colleges talk of it the night before. They discussed it without reserve before him but desired afterwards that he would not mention it. He mentioned the boys I have before noted. After church the boys were desired all to attend in the upper school where all the Masters were assembled. Not one of them had the least idea of what was to happen. Mr Keate called out their names and expelled the Oppidans. He then said that he hoped this measure would be a lesson to them all and a warning to behave better - upon which that disagreeable boy Palk said "Never" - which Mr Drury overhearing said that he could not forbear stating the rebellious expression which he had that minute heard Palk utter. Mr Keate then asked all the Masters if they did not think that such conduct deserved expulsion - which they all agreed to and he was immediately expelled. Mr Keate came and told us of the expulsion just whilst we were dressing to dine at Dr Roberts. Heaven grant that the measure may put an end to the bad spirit which has pervaded so many of them for some time past. Dr Roberts as Vice Provost ad interim expelled the Collegers. I felt very uncomfortable."[197]

On Wednesday 4th November, she recorded:"Pitt has been the chief actor in all this - I am quite amazed that a Colleger should think of risking so much as to join in the rebellion, he has been a great expense and trouble to his father." And again: "All the boys who were expelled deserved it most richly I am sure. May in particular was one of the worst of them.

"Placards were displayed around the town carrying the words - "Floreat Etona - Down with Keate! - Horeat Seditio - Marriott, Elton, Palk, Elton, Jackson, May, Pitt, White. These names will be soundly revenged by all Etonians. Down with the Tyrant! No five o'clock absence! No disrespect to the 6th Form. To Arms - Revenge."[198]

As the rebellion was christened 'Palk's Rebellion' some contemporary writers consider that Palk may have been badly done by and one writes: "Altogether it was one of those follies which can scarcely take place again, but which it is not amiss to record to show how extremely foolish it was."[199]

Johnny May was expelled from Eton and crept back to Ottery with his tail firmly between his legs.

The event was to have such a profound impact on the lives of father, son and their friends that lengthier extracts from the contemporary correspondence are reproduced which express the deep feelings of all concerned.

George Coleridge wrote to John on November 8th:

"My dearest friend

"It was not till this morning that I was informed of the whole amount of your affliction about your son. John Coleridge (and partly he assures me by your desire) has been so good as to detail to me clearly the whole business, and the probable consequences of it. The sorrow, which it has and will still cause you and Mrs May, I partake of in no small degree. I have long been witness to your affectionate sensibility in afflictions of a much less personal nature, and I can only pray to God that such consolation may be administered to your heart from Heaven and from Earth on the present most distressing occasion as to prevent any serious injury to your health or to that of Mrs May - Suffer therefore my most dear Friend every argument that religion or sound reason offer to have its full weight on your mind, that the restoration of your equanimity is the only method of bringing about the wished for change in your Son's conduct.

"For himself, I will not immediately deem the late occurrence (calamitous as it is) to be without its high hope. The materials of self will, which unchecked would probably have been operating by degrees on the moral, religious and civic principles, have been brought to light at this early period accompanied by severe experience. Your equanimity alone will give you the ability to impress and perpetuate the useful effects of such experience, and gradually to super induce that humble and docile state of mind, which is alone fitted for the attainment either of natural knowledge or religious impressions. - Your own equanimity too will allow you to estimate how much of such unreasonable conduct in your Son has been owing to a perversity of disposition in himself; how much in a relaxation of parental authority in yourself: how much in the vortex of example by which he has been swept away to this act: and finally to the confessedly intemperate manner of Dr Keate. - A reasonable, impartial and cool consideration of these matters, acted upon with firmness, may make you see the calamity in a light much less calamitous, and produce at length a conviction that without some such Fever the patient could never have been restored to Sanity - he that with such noxious materials in his habit, has aberrations from right like periodical ulcerations in the natural body, might have attended him to the end of life.

"Next to the conviction that your own equanimity is necessary to turn this calamity to good, is the confidence which you have a right (if any man in the world has) to place on your friends for the future and proper disposal of your Son. I cannot at present estimate by a knowledge of your Son's acquirements or temper, what on the whole is most advisable to be done: but among others my excellent Nephew John Coleridge and your sensible friend Louis Petit, with whom you can personally talk over the matter - men of cool heads, of warm hearts and of decided love for you, will be forward to render you the most substantial advice that can be offered on the present occasion. And I have every hope that before you can announce with your own hand the scene of affliction which you have been witnessing, you will have discovered a future plan of action in which both your reason and affection for your child can acquiesce. To these hopes and expectations let me add my prayers for you and Mrs May's restoration to comfort - and your son's unfeigned sorrow for and conviction of the impropriety of his conduct."[200]

John wrote to George begging him to act as Johnny's tutor. George had to refuse due to his age and health: "Excuse my dearest Friend the honesty and perplexed manner in which I have penned this short letter and believe me, that such is the state of my nerves from the contents of John Coleridge's letter yesterday and yours of today that I have lost all command of myself."[201] The affair was to taint their friendship for a little while.

'Colonel' James Coleridge also wrote encouraging John not to think the worst of his son, "The best Horse may start, & run away; but he must not be condemned, unless he shows a vicious disposition, & gets a bad Habit. Don't therefore condemn poor John. He must and he will (I hope in God) be taught better, & when he has seen his Error, his spirit may in a right direction, carry him through many difficulties." He continued by offering to accommodate Johnny, "Now my kind hearted Wife will be glad to oblige you, by having John here as one of our Family until the end of January," and suggesting a means of continuing his education, James will take him for his Pupil if Mrs Griffiths (whose son now a pupil) has no objection." He finished his letter on a positive note: "Now if you approve of all this, you will have gained time, to look out for a more permanent Situation."[202]

James 'Duke' Coleridge offered to use Johnny's time as profitably as he could during his stay in Devonshire. He set out the programme he used for Mrs Griffith's son: "My present pupil who remains with me till the middle of January reads with me from ten till near 2 then I employ him in composition or analysis at his own house in the evening. The same time I propose to give up to John who shall find no evidence of me wanting to make his time pass as pleasantly and successfully as circumstances and the shortness of the space will allow."[203]

Southey also wrote immediately to his friend on 16th November (the text subsequently edited and sanitised by his son Cuthbert): "I know something of rebellions, and generally suspect that there has been some fault in the master as well as in the boys, just as a mutiny in a man-of-war affords a strong presumption of tyranny against the captain. Without understanding the merits of this case, it is easy to perceive that the boys believed their privileges were invaded, and fancied that the Magna Charta of Eton was in danger, (The habeas Corpus in schools is in favour of the governors - a writ issued against the subject, and affecting him *in tail*), - took the patriotic side, acting upon Whig principles. They are very good principles in their time and place, and youth is a good time and school a good place for them. When he grows older, he will see the necessity of subordination, and learn that it is only by means of order that liberty can be secured . . .

"I have a fellow feeling for ---- [Johnny?], because I was myself expelled from Westminster, not for a rebellion (though in that, too, I had my share), but for an act of authorship. Wynn, and Bedford, and Strachey (who is now chief secretary at Madras), and myself, planned a periodical paper in emulation of the Microcosm. It was not begun before the two former had left school, and Bedford and I were the only persons actually engaged in it. I well remember my feelings when the first number appeared on Saturday, March 1, 1792 . . . for I was expelled for the fifth number. The subject of that number was flogging, and Heaven knows I thought as little of giving offence by it as of causing an eclipse or an earthquake . . . And for this I was privately expelled from Westminster, and for this I was refused admission at Christ Church, where Randolph, from the friendship which he professed for my Uncle, could not else have decently refused to provide for me by a studentship . . .

"My dear John May, I have got into a strain which I neither intended nor foresaw. Misfortunes, as the story says, are good for something. The stream of my life would certainly have taken a different direction if I had not been expelled, and I am satisfied that it could never have held a better course."[204]

'Johnny' was taken under the Coleridge family wing at Ottery and shared living accommodation. with another student in a cottage. His tutors were James Duke principally with assistance from Francis George and Edward Coleridge (Fellow and Master of Eton). 'Colonel' James again reported to John on 6th December, 1818, "John May is fully as good and kind a Lad as I expected - He is more conformable to our quiet habits of living than I had reason to think he would be. In his Temper he is very even, and in his Manners, Gentlemanly and Attentive: he seems happy and in his Health there is nothing to be wished for; and his Spirits are abundant.

"I conceive the points to be mended are these. He wants a Literary Emulation. - He is satisfied when he does his Task, and glad when he has done - he would be pleased to have James absent for a week and does not yet see the value of the present passing hours. But all this must be conquered - other habits must be acquired; and I hope by the joint efforts of James, Frank and Edward, that we may give him other views and then his natural Talents will push him forward in a better Course and with a better Object in view. I shall also endeavour to give him a more correct Idea of your value of Money of which he is at present so careless. James will prepare him for receiving the Sacrament at Xmas and I can assure you that he is well disposed to view Religion in its proper light. It will afford you pleasure and Mrs May also, to hear that he has gained a good footing in Mrs Coleridge's affections; and I can truly say he is affectionate to me. So far therefore all goes well and to our Heart's Content."

He then told John that Charles Griffiths, the fellow pupil who shared Johnny's cottage, was to leave by the New Year and Johnny would have all of his tutor's attention. He also suggested further tuition: "I have been thinking whether you would like John to have occasional lessons in Arithmetic - there is a good Master here and also a good Drawing Master, he has spare time to attend to both?"[205]

By the end of December James Duke was less than sanguine about the arrangements. He expressed his doubts and justification to John. He was worried that his own health might let him down and the effect this might have upon Johnny. His first duty was to the Church and to his family and, as his present Curacy did not pay much, he would have to look for a more substantial Living. This might also affect Johnny. He was concerned that if he did carry on, Johnny's present place of abode was not satisfactory. Johnny was lodging at a Mr Love's house and as Mr Love was out a lot he was not properly supervised. He expressed his fears regarding Johnny's sense of responsibility: "Who whether we consider his age or his peculiar disposition is very unfit to live in any house without close supervision." He continued: "He is moreover thoughtless, high spirited, and very lively and averse to study and though patient of reproof, forgetful of it also." James Duke impressed upon John May that it would be "a very dangerous thing to permit John to be anywhere but in the house of a very steady watchful clergyman." Johnny had apparently shown no remorse for, or understanding of, what he had done and James Duke despaired how he could keep an eye on Johnny all the time and fulfil his obligations to John May.

John May had also asked James Duke to get the truth out of his son as to what had happened at Eton. Johnny maintained that he had told his father the truth and that it was all in his written statement that he had given to his father.

A post script was added by James Coleridge: "taking into consideration John's character . . . am sorry to tell you that nothing presents itself neither do I seriously advise that he be trusted to board in any house but the one his Master also lives in . . . I ought also to tell you that he has taken a very great fancy to associate with our Vicar's daughter of his own age."[206]

Robert Southey also wrote in December helping his friend to justify Johnny's actions: "I was truly glad to be assured by your last letter, of which I had before suspected, that John had been more sinned against (than) sinning. Indeed by what I have since learned it appears that the master acted at the beginning with great imprudence. If, as has been stated, he ordered the boys to be locked up an hour earlier than usual, because some of them employed their time improperly, it was assuredly an act of injustice towards all the others; & any person who knows what boys at a public school are, ought have anticipated the consequences. In reality one of the best things belonging to public schools is that they generate that kind of spirit, which is liable to explode upon such occasion, but which gives a master who knows how to direct it, the best hold upon his boys. In my time at Westminster if any offence had been committed by some unknown person, when it was thought necessary to discover and punish, nothing more was necessary than to send one of the monitors around to the different forms, & ask who had done the thing, - & immediately the offender stood up and avowed himself.

"The master behaved injudiciously at first, & his conduct towards John has been abominably unjust. How surely might it have happened that such a punishment might ruin a boys fairest prospects; - for instance if instead of having a good and affectionate father, his fortune depended upon the will of some relation who without inquiring into the merits of the case, might think it a sufficient reason for discarding him, because he had been expelled from school. Public expulsion is for this reason too severe a punishment for anything except some heinous moral offence. - But boys are as tractable when they are treated justly, & generously & kindly, that Dr. Bell says it is almost always the masters fault if they require punishment at all."[207]

On February 1819 and whilst still at Heath's Court, Johnny realised that to see his father again he would need to make amends. He wrote an abjectly contrite letter to his father begging his forgiveness:-
"My beloved Father

"A long time has elapsed since I last wrote to you, and hearing from my kindest friend Colonel Coleridge, that you are unwell, which he thinks is occasioned by the sorrow and grief I have been the author of to you, I think it now my duty to alleviate you as far as is in the power of a truly penitent son, and one truly sorrowful for the crime he has committed. I know, my beloved Father, that the letter which I am about to write can only intimate to you my sorrow and determination to amend and, I hope and trust that you will think, and by thinking so, alleviate your grief, that this determination will be put into effect. You must naturally suppose how unhappy your last letter made me.

"To think that I was now at variance with that Father, who has endeavoured every thing in his power to make me a good Christian, and a happy man, and sorry I am to say, that I frustrated all his endeavours:

but I still hope and trust in God, that there is yet a chance of my profiting by them, and I humbly beseech him to give me this grace and assistance that I may be able to seize this chance and apply it to myself. Every morning and evening I fervently pray to the Almighty to keep and assist me; and as often do I meditate on your's and my dearest Mother's situation; I often wonder within myself "to know" what induced me so to disgrace myself, and bring misery to my dearest friends. How often do I now wish myself back at Eton! How often do I know, but too late contemplate on the cursed foolish part I then acted! but alas! I can now no more view that sublime place with any comfort! Yet altho' I cannot view it with any comfort or pleasure , yet I am able to think of it with sorrow and pain! but added to this folly, my last crime suffers me to have no peace within myself: I am unhappy where ever I go, and altho' I sometimes forget myself, yet before a short time has elapsed all my unhappiness rushes down upon me like a torrent: on a sudden I remember my beloved Family, who, at the time, I am unjustly enjoying myself, are in the deepest grief and pain: but what most harasses and torments me is the knowing, that I have not obtained your pardon: I have heard of your frequent intentions to come down to Ottery and as often has fresh misery come upon me for how can I dare, much less bear, to meet a Father, I have so shamefully, so scandalously treated? With what a countenance can I meet you? Can I speak to you! At this moment I say I cannot: Instead of looking forward to your visit with joy, and gladness, I shall meet it with sorrow and pain: Meet it! did I say; I do not think I can dare to meet you.

"O! how unhappy! How miserable! must that Son be, who is afraid to meet his own parent! But such is the case with me. I must meet you; but I do not know how to do so. Then, my beloved Father, do I beseech you grant me your pardon and forgiveness: I promise faithfully never to do the like again, I shall be unhappy and miserable if you will not grant it to me. I see my folly, my wickedness; and I will with God's help heartily repent and amend. Be not wroth against me, but pardon me.

"I now see all my faults, I hope, in the right way. I see how extremely backward I am in my learning, and therefore will most zealously endeavour to make up for lost time: I will not idle away my time in folly and buffoonery: but I will steadily apply my shoulders to the plough and work hard to gain the fields I have neglected in fine; I will so work, that you may, at any rate, when you come down find that I am improved: I hope; and I think I am doing so.

"As to my conduct I will so regulate it, that Colonel and Mr James Coleridge may be able to give you a good account of me: and then I shall hope to meet you more composed, altho' it will then be in misery. I shall be happy when I am once reconciled to you all again: it will be unhappiness to me to meet you. I cannot say more than I have done, and I again repeat, that "I am sorry for what I have done, and I will repent and amend. I beseech you, my dearest Father, to have compassion on me, and forgive me! I am unhappy, and most assuredly shall not be otherwise until I receive yours' and my distressed Mother's forgiveness. I have read Bishop Horne's Sermon on Repentancy and have twice written on the same subjects, and I will endeavour to act up to what I have written, and follow what I have read. "Repent and be forgiven". I do most heartily repent: I openly confess every thing that I so shamefully committed, I stand corrected; and I resolutely determine to amend; I seek for the forgiveness, and trust that I shall not fail in obtaining it.

"Every little enjoyment that I partake, whether it is at home, or abroad, is always intermixed with the recollections of my past offences: my beloved family are constantly in my thoughts, and I do not know how to alleviate their grief; I write, but that is only stating things, that are to come: but yet I entreat and beseech you all to depend upon my promises: they shall not be vain ones, but shall be productive in every way: I can not say more. I will work hard, as I said before, to make up for lost time, I will "so run, that I may obtain" I will as readily as I can adhere to the right path, and fight against every thing that opposes me: but you cannot expect to receive from me now so much; as if I had not lost any time: I have been acting the part of the Servant, who received one talent from his master, and who made no use of it, but hid it in the earth, where it increased not but was the same as when he put it there; but with God's assistance I will now act the part of the Servants, who were entrusted with ten and five talents, and increased them, and brought to their master double which he gave them.

"Thus, my beloved Father, have I determined to act, and will most certainly put my determinations into effect, after which I shall with joy receive your's and the rest of my beloved family's kindness with joy and comfort: but I once more, before I conclude this part of my letter, earnestly implore your's and my dear Mother's pardon: and beg of you to comfort yourselves, and rely upon everything that I have here declared.

It comes from my heart. - I cannot say any thing more on this point, but I shall not close my letter, before I have mentioned how very kind and affectionate everyone is to me. Colonel Coleridge makes me as happy as he possibly can, but he cannot make me really enjoy myself, while I am so continually fighting against myself; my Conscience tells me that I have sinned, and therefore pleasure, altho' it may for a time, yet it cannot long, stifle my unhappiness: it will sometimes rush forth in the midst of any enjoyment or pleasure I am partaking of, which soon puts a check to it. Mr James Coleridge takes every possible pains to instruct me, in the right path, as likewise to make me a good Scholar, which pains I hope I shall not throw away, like I have done all your kind endeavours. I am aware it entirely depends upon myself, and therefore I shall steadily endeavour henceforward to act my part. To conclude, I am as happy, as one can make me, and pains are taken on the part of every one to make me more so, but I cannot say in any way truly happy.

Give my hearty love and duty to my beloved Mother and Sisters and to all around you, and believe me,
my dearest father.
Your unhappy, but truly penitent Son,
John May

Pray write soon."[208]

The same month James Duke offered his services as a full time tutor for Johnny in Devon, whether or not he obtained another Living.[209] Also in February John had sought advice from John Taylor Coleridge concerning Mr Robinson, a tutor at Eton who charged £200 per annum.[210]

In the first week of March, John, seeing some sense of contrition in his son's behaviour, travelled to Ottery to meet him. They travelled together to Fair Mile where the father caught the coach back to London and Johnny rode over to Sidmouth before returning to Ottery. The meeting had gone well and Johnny's letter home on 8th March is in a much lighter vein. Apparently, however, all was not forgiven as he had not received any letter from his family on that day, his birthday. On 31st March after the meeting, James Duke was able to tell his father that, "His attention to studies has much increased since your visit to Ottery," and "His Devonshire visit cannot be said to have been unprofitable to him."[211]

Early in April, 1819, Johnny left the sanctuary of Ottery and travelled home to Richmond via Eton where Mr and Mrs James

Coleridge, together with Fanny, alighted. James gave John a final report concerning his son: "Your son will have told you of our night walk to view Bath and by one way or another he viewed the best and largest part of Bath. I shall be extremely glad to hear that you have got an eligible situation for him; for he cannot afford to lose any time; to go as he ought, properly prepared to the University. I am satisfied that he considers many essential points, with more seriousness and more consideration of their importance than he did: but this must constantly be impressed on his mind and he must if possible be taught to consider as of less consequence, certain things which he now attaches too much weight in the scale of his Happiness - All matters concerning the Theatres and public performances - Delight in eating and such like Personal pleasures are among those matters to which he discourses with such eagerness and delight as leaves a bad impression on persons not knowing the goodness of his Heart. I mention these matters, perhaps trifling in themselves, but if indulged in leading to a system of personal indulgence that may destroy the wholesome principle of self - denial which is the virtue of humility. I consider as the two foundations on which a good character should be built.

"John is ever ready to oblige and to forgo a pleasure to please any person. - He is ready to promise and means to perform, but I should add that he needs watching - and when ever from Restraint and in full spirits he is apt to become exuberant in conversation, speaking too much and with too little regard to the persons he addresses.

"Experience and attention will I trust cure these defects and I have thought it right to mention all and every defect that have appeared to me, because I know you wish it and because they are not weighty, or incurable, and also because my regard for him, makes me anxious about his well doing.

"My wife and Edward and Fanny all desire to be affectionately remembered to you and Mrs May and to John and pray include my affectionate regards being always truly yours

James Coleridge"[212]

On 17th April, James Duke was sufficiently impressed with Johnny's progress as to offer to become a full time tutor to him until the time he went up to Oxford, probably two years away. He realised however that John was considering the services of a Mr Buckland. John May was under enormous pressure during this time and in November

Edward Coleridge, in apologising for being late in repaying a sum of money, adds in his defence: "Last Easter when we met in John's chambers I had the money in my hands to give it to you but was restrained from so doing by your leaving the room in so much distress about Johnny after your conversation with my Tutor."[213]

George Coleridge now moved to repair the strained relationship between John and himself. He wrote a long letter gently chiding John and recalling the length and depth of their friendship: "At the time, when your grief was fresh, you may recollect that I hastened to anticipate the development of your feelings by a letter; and to calm, if possible, in some small degree, the storm, which had been so unhappily raised in your breast. At that moment, in particular, could I possibly have offered you in my own Person a substantial substitute for your disappointment in the plan of education for your son, I should then most undoubtedly have done it."

He suggested that: "We may agree to let the matter be, as if it had not been." His approach bore fruit and the strength of the friendship ensured that it continued into the future. George was not quite so complimentary about Johnny as James had been and was probably more honest. Regarding Johnny's stay at Ottery, he continued: "After his arrival however and from that time till his final departure I had opportunities from the family at Heath's Court and from his Instructor of hearing such instances of misconduct from the former, of contentious and ignorance from the latter, that in the capacity of a friend, I could no longer withhold information, which whatever pain it might cost, might give you a clearer insight into his conduct and better regulate your mode of providing for his future welfare. Altho' I supposed that both my Brother and Mr James Coleridge had given you reason to suppose that neither his time or duties had been very profitably used during his residence at Ottery yet I concede that delicacy to your feelings might have suppressed matters that could alone make an impression on a tender Parent: and what as a faithful friend, I considered myself bound in duty to reveal. If in so doing, I neither overchanged the accounts which I had received, nor did it from any other motive than Love to you and benefit to your son."[214]

Robert Southey acknowledged the reconciliation between father and son in September, 1819, writing: "I shall hope to see Johnny in the winter."[215] Earlier in the year John had offered to be godfather to Southey's son, Cuthbert, born in February. The offer was declined as arrangements had already been made with Bedford and Wynn.[216]

By November, 1819, Johnny had once again landed himself in trouble and John Taylor Coleridge wrote a lengthy letter to John discussing the two possibilities open to him. The first was to send Johnny back to Ottery. The second was to employ Dr. Arnold as a tutor. "For what is to come I shall freely offer you such considerations as suggest themselves to me. Assuming that you are not discouraged by what has appeared but determined to try every chance for poor Johnny's restoration and well doing according to your former view of him, the doubt lies between James and Arnold, subject in the latter case to the hesitation in his letter. From what has dropped from James in his letter to Fanny and the strong opinion expressed both by him and my father here before now against the Ottery plan, I own I doubt the eligibility of that plan more than ever. My doubts now are independent of John himself. They regard the other parties concerned. It is quite clear that that their minds are made up most strongly against it." John Taylor advised that: "You have to break a habit, and it seems imprudent to put him in a situation where the habit might have daily opportunity of being exercised." John was of course concerned about the financial implications of employing a tutor and was advised by John Taylor that although Dr Arnold charged £500 per annum, some £200 per annum more than John paid at present, this might be offset if Arnold could be persuaded to take on another pupil as well. He tried to salve John's conscience concerning his other children by pointing out the really serious position Johnny was in: "Whoever looks at all the circumstances must see that it is no common case and requires no common remedy. - You may give a moderate sum to some other man and utterly waste it. The boy is either to be cured now by uncommon attention and skill or you will never have a day's happiness with him more." So seriously did John Taylor Coleridge view the situation that he told John he would rearrange his own financial affairs to repay his loans from John within a period of six months if necessary.[217] In, 1819 John Taylor had decided to leave special pleading and come to the Bar, joining the Western Circuit. He had been enabled to do this by a further loan of £1000 made by John.

The decision was made for Johnny to proceed with his education under Dr. Arnold at Laleham, near Staines, until the spring of 1823. He was one of the earliest private pupils at the establishment, which had been set up in 1819 before Dr Arnold had become headmaster of Rugby or purchased Fox How in Rydal.[218]

Extract from The Green Ottery Copy book: Note to Monodony on the Death of Chatterton. in A Collection of Poems and Prose by Mr Samuel Coleridge, Transcribed [? John May. Jr.]. 21 ff (S MS F1.3).
By courtesy of Victoria University Library (Toronto).

George Coleridge let John know his approval of the new arrangement. "I was informed of the judicious plan for your Son. I hope his own experience aided by such an able and prudent instructor will have a tendency to induce manly reflections and a desire to excel. The time too, which you have allowed for these good purposes, is liberal, and will indicate most clearly what you are to expect from his future life and in what profession he should move, before it is terminated. The occasions wch bring him home for vacation will furnish you with the best instance of observing his improvement. When restraint is thrown off nature and the fixed habit of thinking and acting then exhibit themselves. I shall be happy to hear from time to time what your opinion is of his progress and of the ability of his Tutor!"[219]

In December, 1820, George Coleridge, referring to John Taylor, wrote, "In mentioning his name, I am resulted to the event of his expected conference with Mr Arnold, your Son's Tutor. I know you were anxious about the result of such conference, reasonably judging that Mr A would be more explicit in his opinion with John than he had been in his report to you."[220] Two years later, in April, 1822, Dr Arnold spoke in the warmest terms of Johnny and said how glad he was to have had him under his care.[221]

Ernest Hartley Coleridge whilst editing Samuel Taylor Coleridges' works suggested that Johnny may have transcribed into 'The Green Ottery Copy-book'[222] a collection of Poems and Prose written by his grandfather in the late eighteenth century. These had then been given to his brother George whilst at Hackney and subsequently passed to John Taylor Coleridge.The probable date of the transcription was felt to have been around 1820.[223]

The comment has been made that the initialled note to the antepenultimate line (line 91/143.1.9) to 'Monodony on the Death of Chatterton' was written by Johnny and another observation that "at about the time the transcription is supposed to have been made, John May Jnr. was paying court to Sara Coleridge,(who in early summer 1823 was in Devonshire)."[224] the inference might be made that the transcription was probably made at that time. Johnny however had left Ottery to return to Richmond in April 1819. He got into some more bother and joined Dr Arnold at Laleham in the winter of the same year where he remained until the spring of 1823. He then proceeded to Exeter College,Oxford. He would only have been at Ottery in 1823 for the vacation, if at all. Dr Arnold worked him hard and on July 3rd, 1820, wrote to Johnny's father suggesting that he should study Modern Geography, Herodotus and Livy rather than run the danger of spending six weeks doing nothing.[225] It is suggested that John May Jr. copied the poems in random order and that "he was a fairly accurate transcriber, but not good at spelling." The comments on spelling would be entirely appropriate to Johnny's Journal written in 1822. It is said that the case for John May, Jr. as copyist rests in part on an endorsement on the manuscript itself, partly on circumstantial evidence of Johnny's whereabouts and partly on authenticated examples of his handwriting which appear to be slightly different from that of the Green Ottery Copy book endorsement. Furthermore that the authenticity could be based upon "family correspondence or tradition which has not survived."

There are many authenticated examples of Johnny May's handwriting from 1819 to 1850 none of which would appear to an untrained eye to be similar to that of the transcription made under 'Monody on the Death of Chatterton' in 'The Green Ottery Copy-book'.His handwriting changed significantly during the period of his life at Oxford University and subsequent curacy. Of the letters specifically referred to as comparisons (Bodleian MS Eng lett c 290 ff 100', 104', 106') the first two written on March 8th, 1819, from Ottery and July 11th, 1828, from Hackney are in the same style as his Journal. The last written on January 1st, 1830, also from Hackney, displays a more open sprawling hand. Given his recent behaviour together with subsequent reports on his time at Ottery, the question must be posed whether he would have been entrusted with actual transcription in 1819 and indeed if his intellectual capabilities and concentration were sufficient at that time?

There remains the accreditation by Ernest Hartley Coleridge suggesting that Johnny may have been responsible for the transcription. E.H.Coleridge, born in 1846, would have been writing at least 40 years after the event and then working from family papers or recollection. The date of around 1820 is close to the period when Johnny was at Ottery with his tutors, a time unlikely to have been forgotten by the family and it is very probable that he worked on the Green Ottery Copy Book as part of his studies overseen by, and possibly assisting, one of his tutors, probably James Duke Coleridge. John Taylor Coleridge was keenly monitoring Johnny's progress and may well have been responsible for passing the manuscripts to Ottery.

John Taylor had also received a school report on behalf of Samuel Taylor Coleridge in respect of his son Hartley Coleridge. In June, 1820, Edward Copplestone gave notice that he was dismissing Hartley from Oriel College for drunkenness, irregular behaviour and keeping low company. Samuel heard the news not from Hartley, but from Dr James Gillman to whom John Taylor had written confidentially on 29th June, 1820. In an attempt to smooth the way for Hartley leaving, the College offered to pay £300 compensation if he would resign. Samuel would not agree to this and fought the College, a contest that ended in his failure and with John Taylor Coleridge acting as an intermediary to accept a final unofficial payment of £300..5..6. Thomas Arnold, who was a member of the Fellows Common Room at Oriel, was austere and not appreciative of pursuits other than the intellectual. Samuel was greatly distressed that Robert Southey was informed of Hartley's dismissal before him.

Whilst experiencing serious troubles in his financial affairs, John May had been able to lend John Taylor Coleridge money to follow his legal career and join the Western circuit. In 1819, he advised his brother,

Joseph, to take out a life insurance of £5000 for the express purpose of contributing towards the payment of his debts to the family estate. The premium was £267.11d per annum.[226] George Coleridge was concerned for John's situation, writing: "That part of your letter wch alludes to your precarious situation in life cannot be otherwise than most interesting to me." He compared his own financial situation with that of his friend: "Competence no doubt is a very uncertain & vague term because ten men in the same rank of life with equal families will, owing to their different habits, modes of education or feelings, differ materially in estimating the quantum for such competence. Five hundred a year for instance, would be a competence for me and Mrs. G Coleridge, where one thousand a year would be but a bare competence for you and Mrs May and this is not altogether imaginary for long habit and as it were being bred in a particular style of livery wealds a sort of necessity".[227] In April, 1820, John became godfather to John Taylor Coleridge's son John Duke Coleridge but was not able to attend the quickly arranged baptism.[228] He also received pleasing news of Johnny's progress at Dr. Arnold's.[229]

Throughout 1820 Southey advised John that his brother William should extricate himself from any dependence upon the Brazilian Government. Clearly he felt that William was acting less than responsibly towards John's overall interests in Brazil, a sentiment that was to be echoed by George Coleridge in 1822. Southey sent the first of his series of seventeen autobiographical letters written to John May on July 26th, 1820. The final one was dated March 16th, 1825.

In the spring of 1820 John considered leaving his wine venture with the Sterts. Edward Coleridge wrote to him: "I have read your Acct of your Wine Concern & of your Intention to separate from it; and as far as my judgement goes (which cannot be a great way) I think you owe it to yourself to clear yourself from the Concern; or at any rate to prevent Mr Stt from the free use he has made of the joint Capital." The plan you have offered seems so fair to him, that I do not see how it can be honestly refused, at least it ought to have his Concurrence! I think the concern, taken simply, may be said to be a thriving one, but if, in addition to each partner taking his Share of the Profit, one of them also takes out part of the Capital as a Debt, and gives no security for repaying such overplus Sum taken; then the Concern must get worse & worse - and of course must cease to be profitable, and can only be saved from Ruin, by a great

Increase of Profit, sufficient to enable the borrower to pay back his Debt, & cease to make a new one. But I know nothing more of those affairs than common sense permits me, & as far as that goes I am very anxious on your Account that you shou'd be clear of it - unless indeed Mr Stert's Friends will come forward & save you harmless.[230] By October, 1820, the partnership had ended with a reasonable balance in John's favour. George and James each transferred £2,000 to John May to help him in his dire straights.[231]

George Coleridge and his wife enjoyed a visit to the Mays at Richmond in June and described the "vehicle that conveyed us from Kensington to Ottery in about 23 hours".[232] The political situation in Brazil was a great cause for concern and in September, 1821, a codicil to his mother's will recites that a sum of £12,000, about £750,000 in today's terms, had been borrowed by her son John May and that he had given her a Bond and Assignment of certain Policies of assurance by way of counter security.[233] This loan was arranged by the setting up of a Trust and was an Encumbrance upon the estate of Hale. It was to have very serious implications in the future. In the same month, whilst praising John's prudence, punctuality, method, and the virtues and habits which the mercantile profession requires, Southey wrote expressing "much anxiety" concerning the way in which the revolutionary movements in Brazil might have affected his fortunes. He sent John a portrait of his goddaughter painted by Nash.[234]

The same year he was able to transfer "£625 in three per cents". He sympathised with John's plight and wished the sum could be more. His son Charles Cuthbert mentions that the letter of December 10th was published "with Mr May's approval, as illustrative of the kindness of my father's heart, the warmth and stability of his friendships, and his grateful remembrance of many similar services rendered to him by his friend in past years."[235]

'The Journal of a Short Tour to the Lakes.'

Southey was always fully appreciative of his friend's earlier benevolence and, wanting to repay this in any way he could, invited him to stay at Greta Hall: "One word more. I entreat you break away from business, if it be possible, as early in the spring as you can, and put yourself in the mail for this place. Though you cannot leave your anxieties behind you, yet you may, by means of change of air and scene, be assisted in bearing them, and lay in here a store of pleasant recollections, which in moods of mind are wholesome."

In 1821 it was arranged that Johnny should proceed to Exeter College, Oxford University, where he was entered on 2nd February, 1822 (Aged 19. A Commoner).[236] George Coleridge wrote on 22nd: "I am happy you have at length entered John May at Exeter. The preparation which he will have had from his excellent Tutor, your solemn statement of your affairs to him (which might as well be resumed at times) and above all his experience of past events, may be auxiliaries to that steadiness and prudence of conduct during his College Residence, which you could not have confidently expected otherwise."[237]

John's Brazilian ventures collapsed entirely early in 1822. He wanted to travel out there to see his brother William who had travelled back to Brazil in 1819 after his marriage. His mother and friends counselled him against such a trip. George wrote on February 22nd: "Of the calamitous situation of your mercantile funds I had heard partly from John Coleridge but in no way in so detailed a form as you have taken the trouble to exhibit them. All we can say my dear friend is this that God knows best what is fitted for us as to time and measure - that we must prepare for the worst and hope for the best. If sorrow could avert or stay the stroke of calamity this would be beneficial, but since it cannot, our constant prayer should be for resignation, not in name or in letter but in reality, from the heart and in Spirit. The resources which the Christian Religion affords you and the health of yourself and dear family are blessings above estimation. A more contracted sphere of life when compulsory has benefits which cannot be contemplated at a distance, and you who have indulged the feelings of benevolence in the most expansive stream in the time of your prosperity, need not fear that the fountain will be dried up although your means are crippled. A man is judged by what he hath, not by what he hath not.

"The hazard to your person, your increased expense from such an adventure and your probable failure after all, with the disgrace entailed on your Brother by such a dependence on his integrity are considerations not to be slighted and I trust that you will be convinced that on the whole the risk is not a duty imperative on you."[238]

James Coleridge had to send John a friendly reminder that a due dividend had not been paid into his account at Russell & Cole. In March

Southey was concerned at not having heard from John and wrote to his brother Henry asking, "Have you seen John May lately? I am anxious to hear how he is going on and not a little apprehensive that his last accounts are unfavourable ones because I have not heard from him."[239]

Johnny could not proceed to Oxford directly; there was a lack of accommodation near the university. The state of his business caused John to make enquiries concerning an alternative school at less expense than that of Dr Arnold's. Again he turned to his friend John Taylor Coleridge who on 31st March, 1822, advised him regarding a new school being set up at Longworth under the care of Rev. John Blackmore: "Sorry as I am for the disappointment there is yet one good to be discovered from it. John will see that a departure from his word is not so wholly unattended with inconvenience as he might have fancied if he had proceeded to immediate admission to Exeter College - and it will not be amiss if he finds himself a little less comfortable at Longworth than he did at Laleham." With regard to Rev Blackmore he advised John that he was now married, has one pupil with another expected and that he hopes to take up to four at a rate of £200 a year.[240]

Hartley Coleridge's drinking and lifestyle deteriorated through 1822 to such an extent that he deserted his father and sick brother Derwent in the summer, spent a while in London and had fled to Ambleside by October. Neither Southey nor Wordsworth would offer him accommodation. He found a room at the Red Lion Inn at Grasmere.

John May sent some Hale 'strong beer' to Southey who was also looking forward to receiving "a barrel of Devonshire cyder" from Ottery to place "on each side of it".[241]

Arrangements for John's visit to Greta Hall and the English Lakes continued through April to July. He decided to take his son with him and Southey expressed delight although accommodation might be tight. He gave some travel hints: "We shall be very glad to see your son with you, & should be more so if we had a bed to offer him. But in all likelihood it will be easy to get him one, at the bottom of the garden, & if not, one of the Inns is within five minutes walk. There are two Carlisle mails, & he who takes the wrong one has to spend three hours at midnight in a Manchester Inn, the worst place on this side of Purgatory. The right one is that from the Bull & Mouth, which goes thro Doncaster. You must take your place to Penrith, which is 18 miles from hence: & You will be here

The old school house, Grasmere.

in 41 hours from London. - When I am once settled in the coach I think nothing of the journey. I should look forward to this meeting with unmingled pleasure, if you would come without a load of cares, & if you could make a longer tarriance.

"As it is I look to it with great delight, & not without hope that things will have brightened by that time (as they are not darkening now) & that you will find your spirits freshened by the visit. Your Goddaughter goes, I believe this week to Harrogate. We shall miss her much - but I am very glad that there is an opportunity of sending her there.

"I hope I shall be near the end of my first volume by the time you come. Indeed it is time I should, because of its length, - & there is little but plain sailing before me. - Something it will enable me to place at your disposal - I heartily wish it were more. I have a great deal to show you, & a great deal to say."[242]

The forthcoming visit meant a great deal to Southey and he expressed his feelings to his uncle, Rev Herbert Hill: "John May talks of paying me a visit in June, though his furlough will only extend to a clear fortnight. There is no person whom I should be more glad to see, except yourself."[243]

The stay had to be postponed a month from June to July due to Robert's illness but on 22nd July Southey again wrote to his brother Henry saying: "I have been looking every day to hear of John May."[244] His patience was rewarded on 25th July with a letter from John to which he replied: "I received your letter this day (Thursday) - on which our post does not go out from London. A letter which should leave Keswick tomorrow would arrive in town on Monday, - but you travel in a day coach, & therefore I can only reach you by firing a shot at Birmingham. There was two years ago a mail from Birmingham to Manchester, which started about ten or eleven in the forenoon. It may probably be earlier now, since the increased celerity of the mail-motions. That mail will bring you to Manchester time enough for the Kendal mail, in which you will have a much better chance of sleeping than in a Manchester Inn & at any rate will pass the night more satisfactorily. It sets out for the Bridgewater arms, & will bring you to Kendal early the next morning, in time for the Keswick Coach. You will reach Keswick by two o clock, & I shall be on the look out for you.

"My old friend Lightfoot whom I was in hopes you would have seen here, will pass thro Birmingham on his return, while you are there. If you will leave a note at the Inn where the Manchester coach puts up, saying where you are to be found, he will be heartily glad to find some one who knows him there by name, & you will see one of the worthiest men in the world, who will give you a full account of us. He is a clergyman, & Master of the Grammer School at Crediton - an old fellow collegian of mine, whom I had not seen for eight & twenty years till now.

"I am in pretty good training at present, & we shall try Johns hand at an oar, & his feet upon the mountains."[245]

In another letter to his uncle Southey says: "I returned from Rydal to-day, not the worse for a walk of fifteen miles, the last ten in the rain. A great deal of exercise during the last three weeks has done me great service, and when John May and his son arrive I shall put them upon their mettle."[246]

On Monday 29 July, 1822, the two John Mays, father and son, left London to travel to Keswick. During their Tour they visited the Soho Works near Birmingham, a visit that made a great impression on Johnny. The Soho Manufactory, as it was called, came about when Mathew Boulton, brought together a number of branches of the toy making trade in one location allowing him to handle the manufacture as well as the selling himself. Up till then the two stages existed separately. Mathew Boulton was born in Birmingham on 3rd September, 1728, the son of a toymaker working from a manufactory next to his house. In those days the word 'toy' referred to small metal objects such as seals, snuff boxes and items we now consider to be jewellery.

In 1761 Mathew entered into partnership with John Fothergill at Birmingham. They found a site with water power just north of Birmingham at Handsworth and each put £5000 into the business. It was an entirely new concept housing many different specialised trades and was a very important part of the industrial revolution. By 1765 the factory had been extended twice. There was a problem however in that the water power was not entirely reliable during the summer months. James Watt developer of the steam engine visited Soho in 1768 on his way from Scotland to London. Boulton saw the potential of Watt's engine and bought out his sponsor's share thus allowing Watt and his engine to move from Scotland to Birmingham. In 1775 Watt obtained an extension of his patent for twenty-five years and entered into partnership with Boulton.

James Watt Junior and Mathew Robinson Boulton, the sons of the original partners, entered the partnership in 1794 and the firm became Boulton, Watt and Sons. By 1800 the manufactory was supplying its coining machinery to the Royal Mint in London and in 1802 the first public exhibition of gas lighting was staged there. The older partners retired and the sons changed the business name to Boulton, Watt and Co. Mathew Boulton died on August 17th, 1809. and James Watt on August 25th, 1819.

The following description was given in a popular guide in the first quarter of the nineteenth century: "In the neighbourhood of this town are the famous Soho works, belonging to Messrs. Boulton and Co., forming one of the most extensive manufactories in the kingdom; as well as for the number of hands it employs, as for the variety of articles it produces. It consists of four squares, with connecting ranges of shops like streets, capable of employing above 1000 workmen in all the varieties of the button, buckle, plated, or argent-molu, steel and trinket manufactory. The improved steam-engines of the late Mr Watt, also made here, deserve to rank among the most extraordinary inventions of the present age."[247]

Mathew's son Mathew Robinson Boulton died in 1842 twenty years after the Mays were introduced to him. By 1848 the manufactory had ceased to operate and in 1863 the site was cleared for a housing estate[248]. In the first quarter of the nineteenth century the manufactory was one of the places expected to be included in the itinerary of an English tour.

Johnny and his father were also to see the sights described to J.J. Morgan by Samuel Taylor Coleridge some ten years earlier: "Near Birmingham I observed a cluster of enormous Furnaces, with columns of flame instead of Smoke from their chimneys."[249]

In Manchester their guide was John Hull, an old Etonian friend who became Vicar of Poulton-le-Fylde, Lancashire; Canon of Manchester and Chaplain to the Bishop.[250]

Johnny kept a Journal of the Tour in a notebook written mainly on one side only of each page. The Journal finishes with their arrival at Robert Southey's home, Greta Hall, on Monday 5th August 1822. The opening comments by young Johnny suggest that the Tour was very important to his father who apart from being extremely keen to see and talk, face to face, with his old friend again, may not by then have been able to afford to send his son further afield. His business situation was desperate but always thinking of family and friends first he will have remembered financing John Taylor Coleridge's 'Grand Tour' of Europe in 1815. The Tour was equally important to Johnny striving still to make amends for past misdemeanours and to prove himself both to Dr Arnold towards the end of his tuition at Laleham and more particularly to his father.

The May's stayed with Robert Southey and his extended family at Greta Hall for four weeks,[251] and left on 2nd September 1822.[252] It was their first and apparently only visit despite the life long friendship enjoyed by the two older men. It was a great success. Reminiscing over the visit Southey was able to tell his Uncle Rev Herbert Hill that "John May enjoyed his visit greatly"[253] and John Rickman "John May came to me just after Lightfoot's departure. I walked about a hundred miles more with him, and am now in as good trim for walking as any man of my years need be." [254]

Father and son had travelled from Rydal to Keswick in the company of a Dr. Bell. He had arrived in Westmoreland to visit Robert Southey had just left Rydal Mount, the home of William Wordsworth. Dr Bell, as has been mentioned, was an enthusiastic exponent of the 'Madras

System' of educational reform. He died on 27th January, 1832, aged 79 and was interred in Westminster Abbey. The inscription on his tombstone reads: "The Author of the Madras System of Education."[255] By 1799 he had introduced the system to Kendal School. He had written letters extolling the topographical virtues of Bassenthwaite and Grasmere: "To those who follow our track, for I would have all summer travellers from your quarter to Manchester or Liverpool take the same course, let me recommend them to step aside one mile from the road to the inn at Ouse bridge, on the northern extremity of Bassenthwaite lake; which, though obscure or little noticed by travellers, is yet deserving of much notice. From the window of the inn, built for this purpose, and from an adjacent bridge, where the lake terminates, is a beautiful prospect, a full view of the commencement of the lakes." Regarding Grasmere he added "He must again turn a quarter of a mile to the right of his road, to an inn and a church, whence he is to view the charming lake of Grasmere." In 1811 the Rev. W. Johnson, then twenty eight years old, curate of the parish of Grasmere and master of its endowed village school, had, with William Wordsworth's encouragement, introduced the Madras System of education to his school.

Dr Bell travelled extensively in England, 1282 miles on horseback in 1812 and over 1300 by the summer of 1813. He visited Grasmere, Keswick and Kendal regularly during the first quarter of the nineteenth century whilst establishing his system in a growing number of schools. Bell was a friend of both William Wordsworth and Robert Southey. In 1812 he 'head hunted' the Rev Johnson to work for him full time in London. Wordsworth acted as Johnson's agent and suitable terms were agreed. The move was marked by Lady Fleming of Rydal Hall, the patroness of the living, who expressed great regret at Mr Johnson's departure and, as a token of her good feeling towards him, presented him with a purse of gold.

After Rev Johnson had left for Holborn, his post as teacher was taken in the spring of 1812 on a temporary basis by a young man named Bamford, then the head boy of the Grammar-school in Ambleside and a colleague of Hartley Coleridge. Mr Bamford provided an illuminating account of Grasmere school life at the time: "The school at Grasmere is situated at the north corner of the church yard. It is a very low, dark, and poor building, though it had been honoured by the children of the greatest poet, and was still attended by the children of many an honest and wealthy Westmoreland yeoman. There was a long flat table, a few forms, and a chair at one end for the master. I had followed the common routine of other country schools. The children came up generally individually four times in the day, and managed, some way or other, to get through as many lessons."[256] The old school building is today occupied by the Gingerbread shop.

In July, having made a visit to Liverpool Dr Bell proceeded northward. Southey recounts in his biography of William Bell "After a passing visit to Mr Wordsworth, he came to Keswick, where he remained in lodgings for a month, passing his evenings, for the most part, at Greta Hall." It was on this visit that he met the Mays.

On the evening of his arrival Johnny was immediately smitten by Sara Coleridge. An affair of the heart started and, totally in character, it seems to have verged upon infatuation on his part. Sara was prepared to end the relationship and accord with the family wishes of both Johnny's father and Robert Southey, neither of whom would bless the union. Their attitude was no doubt based upon the couple's age, Johnny's track record of poor behaviour and Southey's feelings toward Samuel Taylor Coleridge. Southey replied in September to a letter from John concerning the affair. He had decided not to tell Mrs Coleridge of its contents as she had said nothing to either his wife or himself implying, he thought, either that she felt there was "a sense of impropriety in the affair" or that Sara had dismissed Johnny's attentions.[257]

John had written to his friend George Coleridge during his stay at Greta Hall giving him news of the Cumberland branch of the family. When they travelled south again, father and son went to Hale. In September, George gratefully thanked him for his earlier letter and continued, "Any account too of Mr Southey and family is interesting to me as I have a high respect for his Virtues and Principles. The Picture which you had drawn of all the members under his roof is very pleasing and is shaded only by some collateral reflections touching certain Males of the family, whom even the experience of adversity is not likely to reduce to sanity. A shadow too hangs over the pleasing account my Friend gives of the refreshment which he has found from the conversation of Mr Southey and the exhilarating scenery of the Lakes - from the ceaseless and harassing anxiety about his secular matters. Be assured that I cannot be comfortable on your account, as I cannot but dread even the possibility of your being severed from us by the Atlantic. Good God!

- Has your Brother William so lost all natural affection and sense of Justice as to make such a step necessary! Or are his circumstances so embarrassed that in full possession of right feelings he is utterly unable to do what is right? If this latter be ascertained to be the case, what use can there be in risking your person on so hazardous and disgusting an exploit? If indeed you cannot come at any certainty with respect to his situation on this side the water, there may be some reason for personal intercourse. Of this you know best and probably it is folly in me to urge disuasion for your adventure when you are sufficiently disinclined yourself but all events I shall be anxious to hear the results of your family consultation after you have left Hale."

George Coleridge continues: "I presume that John May continues with Mr Arnold till the spring and I have great hopes that the interruption which has prevented his early entering at College will be ultimately very beneficial. I wished when I was 24 years old that I could again have a College education. Nay after my good father was no more and I at College I would gladly again have put myself to School. I was at College before I was 17 and at Hackney before I was 19. I have therefore had an uphill game to play. It has pleased the merciful God however to carry me through without any very horrible miscarriage and has set me down with much more than ever I desired or deserved. Let not John May therefore [rebel] at the delay. I hope the satisfaction which he will afford you by his conduct at College will be a powerful counterbalance to the many anxieties with which you are surrounded."[258]

In October these plans were to be amended. An undergraduate named Jones, well known to John Taylor Coleridge, had written to him informing of the availability of some rooms though harbouring serious doubts about having Johnny to share. "We hear unfavourable reports of him," he said, "but we will not decline to give him a fair trial and his friends must of course be prepared to remove him if he does not succeed." John Taylor told John "On the one hand if I did not think that I could promise for Mr Jones that he would have a fair trial I would not advise him even now to go. On the other I earnestly conjure John to consider the difficulties of his situation and that he has brought it on himself - he may now see how soon man becomes a responsible being and how long the consequences may cling to him of a false step made soon in early boyhood. Let him now once more seriously go over his past life - and see whether he has not at times, when he little thought of the years to come, given occasion to people to settle those unfavourable reports of him which now press upon him in his prospect in life."

He reminded John of the time "when he was thoughtlessly heading a row at Eton, what would he have said, if you or I had told him that years and years after, what he was then doing might be a stone round his neck - and let him be sure, that of his conduct as a boy at Eton has had a strong influence on his interests as a young man at Oxford. - what he does at Oxford will not less affect his advance hereafter. The step he is now taking may decide the whole colour of his future life - if he pass 3 years at the University morally, respectably, profitably he may well hope to live all his life a comfort and honour to himself and his dearest friends, - but the habits of three years are made up of daily acts - an impertinent word to his tutor today, a lecture slurred over today, one drunken party today, one staying out unreasonably late at night - each of these paves the way to the next transgression - and if he come from Oxford unimproved a mere thoughtless, good natured, idle, trifler, what hope can he have of himself - where will he improve, or when, if not there and then?"

"It is John's fault (and I am sure you will forgive me if I think that your unwillingness to pain him has sometimes led you to indulge it in him) it is his fault to forget the past too soon and to rely too much on his own strength. A steady course is not easy for any young man, and John's experience should tell him that for him it is peculiarly hard - that very experience should be his safe guard - whatever we do, let him not forgive or excuse himself - I could wish almost that Eton and Laleham should be words uttered to himself every morning and evening after his daily prayers - Far be it from me to wish to discourage him but he must not disguise to himself the difficulties before him.

"Eyes are upon him from the moment he sets foot in Exeter [College]. They fear Evil for him - what might be overlooked in another, will be recognised as a specimen of old habits in him. I say to him then - Be sober, be vigilant. The moment you find your companion is idle, or unprofitable, wean yourself from him - don't wait till you find him out to be immoral or irreligious, let it be enough for you that he is a trifler.

"Don't wait for John's going till your visit at Hale closes - let him go at once - it will please them."[259]

Southey alluded to 'the affair' in a letter to John at the end of the year. He told John that Sara and Mrs Coleridge had left on a tour, staying a month in Derby, moving on to Clarkson's near to Ipswich for

Christmas, on to Highgate and "lastly to Somersetshire to visit Poole, and then to Ottery, if they are invited. . . . It may be prudent for you to manage that Sara's visit to John Coleridge does not take place during a vacation; - they can have no other opportunity of meeting; - & as matters now are, on this side at least, you may then be perfectly at ease. She is heart whole, - the affair never gave her half the uneasiness it did you. John, I dare say, will fall in at Exeter, with the son of my good friend Lightfoot. - My name will naturally draw them together. I have never seen young Lightfoot, but from all which I have heard of him, his sterling qualities would render him a valuable acquaintance for John - if they should take to each other."[260]

Sara visited her father Samuel Taylor Coleridge at Highgate on this journey. Two of her cousins, one being Henry Nelson Coleridge, also arrived on 29th December, 1822. Henry and Sara were soon secretly engaged. "Sara and myself", Henry wrote in his diary for 21st March 1823, "are solemnly engaged to each other. She has promised never to marry any one but me". Sara and Henry knew that their engagement would be of a long duration and were careful to keep it secret, for they feared the interference of their families."[261] It would seem that she had soon forgotten Johnny's attentions!

The ladies continued their journey to Ottery St Mary to stay with the Devon branch of the Coleridge family. 'The Colonel' was much impressed. "Sara is indeed a sweet creature, and she has attached herself to me, and indeed to us all. Fanny is delighted with her."[262] Mrs Coleridge related to her friend Thomas Poole: "You will I am sure be pleased to hear that our visits at Highgate and Ottery have been productive of the greatest satisfaction to all parties - I shall have a great deal to tell you when we meet, which I hope nothing will prevent..."[263] John Taylor Coleridge was also a member of the house party and thus fully acquainted with the situation.

Johnny May, however, continued his attentions to Sara, when she returned to Keswick in the June of 1823. This worried both Mrs Coleridge and Robert Southey. He wrote again to Johnny's father: "I must now tell you what Mrs Coleridge told him (Edward Coleridge) in my presence & no doubt with the intention that I should hear it, tho she has never at any time spoken a word to me on the subject, nor even hinted at it. Upon mention of your son's name, she told him that he was then in North Wales, & that he talked of coming to this place; - an

Extract from Johnny May's Ordination Papers.
By courtesy of Norfolk Record Office.

intention which I find he has communicated to Sara by letter, a few days ago. - This you will at once perceive places me in a difficult situation. I think if your opinion upon this point had undergone any change, you would have informed me of it, - and unless I were assured that this attachment on his part had now received your approbation; I should feel myself acting very culpably in entertaining him here, & affording him those opportunities which can only be had by being under the same roof with her. Yet on the other hand it will be very unpleasant, - not to say painful, - to receive him coldly & repulsively. That he has continued to write to her is now evident. What encouragement he has received I know not. - Tell me how I am to act, - if there should not be time for you to prevent the visit - I did not expect this perseverance on his part. - & had his attentions been discontinued I am quite certain that Sara would long ago have felt herself disengaged. An expectant attachment of this nature may often I believe be highly useful to the man, as giving him the surest of all preventatives against the greatest danger which lies in the way of youth. But it is not so on the woman's part. Enough of this - & I am afraid too much for your comfort."[264] Edward Coleridge had arrived to stay at Greta Hall at the end of July to enjoy the boating and walking with the guide William Bird on the Wastwater tour.

Sara spoke of Johnny in desperation in a letter to her friend Elizabeth Crump: "Young Mr May wrote to me several times after I saw you and spoke positively of coming to Keswick after visiting Wales to my great annoyance. He is not yet come and I hope that he has given up his plans as I discouraged it in my letter to him and did not answer his last to me. I hope he will make up his mind to forget me and will meet with some one who will make him happier than I could do."[265]

Johnny did not easily give up his quest. Mrs Coleridge told her friend Thomas Poole: "In respect to that affair of her own, of which I gave you a hint in the spring the youth will persevere, and now affects to think himself ill used: he now wishes to keep up a correspondence as Brother & Sister, she has not replied to the two last letters."[266] Young Johnny's continued persistence proved so agitating to Sara and her mother that she accepted John Taylor Coleridge's offer of assistance and requested him "to put an end to the affair in whatever way you judge to be the most conciliating and judicious."[267]

Henry Nelson Coleridge meanwhile went to Ottery where he sought his father's approval of his engagement to Sara. The Colonel flatly refused to give his blessing and demanded that the couple entirely break off any understanding with one another. "To Sara he could, of course, have no justifiable objection. He had grudgingly contributed to Hartley's college expenses, and as far as he was able, lent assistance to the others. But for his son, who was still far from independent, to consider marriage with the penniless daughter of the ne'er-do-well Sam seemed preposterous."[268]

Sara descended into a deep depression that affected her eyes. In November, 1823, Dorothy Wordsworth wrote to Catherine Clarkson: "Poor Sara Coleridge has a weakness in her eyes - very distressing for one of her habits." In September, 1824, she wrote to Lady Beaumont telling her that Sara had ridden over from Borrowdale and that, although she could not detect any ailment to her eyes after examining them, yet Sara said they were very uncomfortable and she could stand a strong light. She was extremely thin and "I could not but think of a lily Flower to be snapped by the first blast, when I looked at her delicate form, her fair and pallid cheeks."[269]

Without doubt, as both this affair, the writings in his Journal and his interest in the Parson's daughter at Ottery show, Johnny had both an eye for the ladies and a rebellious streak to his character. George expressed his concerns to John in August 1823: "Let me now ask you how you think Johnny is really going on - for I wish to have your approbation of him grounded on your own proof and observation," and again, "I must hope that his progress in his learning is manifest and that at least he meets your wishes and circumstances in his College expenses."[270] Johnny seems eventually to have admitted defeat in this love quest and by 1824 turned his attentions to his studies at Oxford, possibly remembering his filial duties and the past events at Eton and Laleham.

1822 - 1900

In August John had found himself in danger of drowning at Brighton. George thanked "Almighty God for your wondrous preservation from so perilous a situation."

The following year at the other end of the country Robert Southey and Professor Sedgwick together witnessed and recorded a rising of the 'Floating Island' on Derwentwater, a phenomena of great interest at the time.[271]

John's business was collapsing in 1822 and Johnny's grandmother, Mary, offered to help the family financially by giving her interest in The Wick to his father in 1823. The house was then thought to be worth around £5000. John although very keen to own it turned the offer down as he thought it should remain in the asset bank of the family as a whole. Mary died in 1824 and the lease of the house passed to John by inheritance. The situation continued to be dire through 1824 when Southey enquired about accounts from Brazil and by 1825 the business had collapsed entirely and John was bankrupt. He looked for employment by the County Receivership, the Commissioners and Comptrollers Office and various Charitable Institutions. Southey advised his friend "to look about, & put out feelers in all directions."[272]

Johnny seems to have taken little notice of the financial situation writing to his father from Holywell, Oxford in October to tell him that his tutor had changed which would cost Father more money but that he had very comfortable lodgings with his friend Pocklington at a rent of a

St John's Hackney, c1830.

guinea a week and that he was "up every morning by seven from which time to four o clock I am hard at my books, breakfast time excepted. - I resume the labour again at eight and continue at it till eleven when I go to bed."[273]

He obtained his B.A. on 8th December[274] and, flushed with success, wrote to his father: " 'Labor omni a vincit.' I have this day finished my examination in the schools - and I am happy to be able to inform you that I have come off with flying colours - I had no idea that it was in my power to do as well as I did, but so it is. I am told and assured that I did very well indeed and my tutor informed me that my Logic Examination was one of the best that has been passed this term. - Be, however, that as it may, the examination is over, and I have with credit to myself and College finished my career at Oxford. - It is, my dear father, with heartfelt joy that I acquaint you with my success, as I know how happy it will make you to hear of it."[275] He went on to explain that the success would cost him another £112 in fees for the degree, his lodgings and his tutor all of which of course he looked to his father to pay!

John, always interested in his son's future and no doubt to ensure against his slipping back to old habits, had written to John Keble, fellow of Oriel College Oxford, one of the leaders of the 'Oxford Movement' and also examiner and tutor at Oxford until 1823, asking his advice regarding appropriate study material that Johnny should read in preparation for his chosen profession. Dr Keble suggested that Johnny might work with sick and elderly people to understand them and no doubt learn humility. He also referred him to Bishop Wilson's works and gave advice regarding sermons. [276]

From January to June Johnny spent his time meditating on his feelings and calling to Holy Orders, relaxing and enjoying some quality time with his father in Boulogne. He also passed several days in Oxford with friends. At the start of June he intended to travel from Oxford to London and from there to Dover and Boulogne from where he could meet up again with his father. On his arrival at Tavistock Street a letter awaited him from Barnard Hanbury, the incumbent of Bures St Mary, Suffolk. Mr Hanbury offered him a curacy from July till November 1826 explaining that the living was a very poor one at £26 a year with the vicarage. He went on to say that, although there was little time before the next ordination, "Still, however, as I have some personal knowledge of the Bishop and a very particular friend is intimate with him I do not despair of getting over this difficulty should we be able to arrange other matters."[277]

Johnny immediately visited his close friend and mentor John Taylor Coleridge who advised him he would lose nothing by taking the post. Time was of the essence as his ordination was to take place on Sunday, 18th June, and he had to attend at Norwich before hand for examinations. He felt very much alone in the world as he followed his decision to carry on into the church. His papers of application as a deacon were signed as displayed in May and June followed by those to become a priest in October, 1826.[278] He accepted the position at Bures, initially for a year, also agreeing to act as tutor for one of Mr Hanbury's pupils at a salary of £150 per annum. St Mary Bures Parish then had a population of 1100. Subsequent letters suggest his curacy at Bures was a very happy period in his life and that the congregation was larger than he had expected, 1500 to 2000 he wrote later, though this may have been an exaggeration brought on by unhappiness in another post. Johnny was at last growing up and as he wrote to his father in June "The responsibility that I am taking upon myself in going into the Church never came across me, accompanied with such intense feelings as it does at the present moment. With God's help I will endeavour to do my duty and with this determination do I start. May God help me!"[279]

John May was experiencing the pains of bankruptcy. In January 1826, Southey commiserated with his predicament in having "to begin the world again, & cast about to retrieve fortunes which have been wrecked by no error or improvidence of your own, is a trying case."[280] John May was now reduced to seeking paid employment with references. In April he mentioned that he was considering applying for a position in a new bank branch that was to be opened, a proposition his friend supported whilst commenting on this fairly new phenomenon.[281] In July, Southey repaid some of the favours he had received in the past and told John that he had received a letter from Miss Bowles to whom he had written regarding a post in the Liverpool Branch Bank. She had obtained promises from Mr Manning and Sir John Reid to mention John's name to the directors.[282] George Coleridge wrote in August; "Among the temporal affairs that at times arrest my thoughts, is your situation, and the wish, the hope, the prayer that you may at length be enabled so to arrange your worldly matters, as to retire from the busy scenes of life to domestic quiet, studious care, and religious composure."[283] William May again left Brazil early in 1826 and Southey commented that this "will not it is hoped delay the liquidation of your debt."[284]

Lord Coleridge, writing about John Taylor Coleridge, comments of this time: "John May, a wine merchant, a friend of the family, lived in affluent circumstances at Richmond. His generosity was often employed in pecuniary assistance by way of gifts and loans. In aftertimes, when financial misfortune overtook him and the family were in more prosperous circumstances, it is pleasant to think that this generosity was amply requited." [285]

From the autumn of 1826 to the spring of 1827 John still hoped for a post at the bank and was weighing up the choices of Bristol, Liverpool or Leeds. By September he was so certain that he was to go to Liverpool that John Taylor Coleridge bemoaned the probability that they would not see much of each other as "I cannot flatter myself that I should often see Liverpool."[286] In May he had decided upon Bristol[287] and by September, 1827, having sold both The Wick at Richmond and 4 Tavistock Street, had moved there. The Bank of England opened a branch at 3 Bridge Street on 12th July and John became the first agent at a salary of £1,000 per annum. He lived at 38 York Crescent, Clifton, whilst the sub-agent

Robert Morris lived in the Bank House, Bristol.[288, 289]

Southey did his best to help his old friend settle into his childhood town introducing him to John King as "John May, who is one of my oldest and best friends . . . I wish you would call upon him and introduce yourself."[290] He wrote to John in September: "I can very well enter into the melancholy part of your feelings upon this transplantation to a strange city, though that city is to me the place in the world, as far as mere place can go, where I should feel myself most at home. Where is your bank, and where your dwelling house? Tell me, that I may see them in my mind's eye when I think of you. I never thought to have seen Bristol again; but, now that you are there, I may find in my heart to revisit it, and show you the houses where my childhood and youth were passed. You ought to become acquainted with my old friend Joseph Cottle, the best hearted of men, with whom my biographical letters one day have much to do. It would give him great pleasure to see any one with whom he could talk about me. Make an hour's leisure some day and call upon him, and announce yourself to him and his sisters as my friend. You will see a notable portrait of me before my name was shorn, and become acquainted with one who has a larger portion of original goodness than falls to the lot of most men."[291] John became close friends with the Cottles until his death.

Early in 1828 John May received the sad news of his friend George Coleridge's death. James Coleridge commented, "I believe the Exeter Physicians hastened poor George's Death."[292] His health had been deteriorating since July of the previous year when John Taylor informed him that the doctors "considered him in a declining state of great danger."[293]

Johnny was also moving home. He left Bures and had joined his family at Clifton near Bristol by April 1828. His health had suffered, probably from a bad attack of smallpox. John Taylor Coleridge was extremely concerned for John's sisters and asked whether they had been revaccinated and what were the appearances. He was glad to see that the family were settling into their new life in Clifton: "I think your account of Mrs May and your dear girls was upon the whole a comfortable one. I am truly glad that the girls have so much innocent amusement in the Society of Clifton though I dare say when the evening comes you are not easily moved out of your chair to a soiree. John had previously written to him expressing concern regarding Johnny's future prospects. John Taylor counselled patience: "You must not forget how young he is at present in a profession which seldom presents a rapid road to competence." He had not thought it advisable to speak to the bishop yet regarding patronage but hoped to be staying with him soon at Farnham Castle when, as he owed it to John May, he hoped to mention it. He was not hopeful of an early result. In fact, the stay did not occur. He went on to urge Johnny to: "Follow up on the plan I suggested of getting into some situation of extensive professional usefulness."[294] During his stay at Clifton, Johnny became engaged to a young lady by the name of Ellen.

By the end of June, John Taylor had used his connections for Johnny to become curate to Mr Norris at the Chapel of St John of Jerusalem in Hackney. The chapel had close links with the 'Great Church' of St John-at-Hackney. When he arrived he was very lonely and disheartened. He quickly formed the impression that there would be little to do and wrote first to Ellen and then to his father: "Mr Norris is very kind to me in every respect and certainly strives, which I am duly sensible of, to make everything as pleasant to me as possible. From all that I can learn from him, my duty here will be any thing but laborious, for altho' the district assigned to his superintendence is large, the demand, as it appears to me, upon the services of the curate is but small: as a proof of which, there is no one at this moment in need of being visited, or in any way requiring the assistance of the clergyman. He himself says that he knows but some of his parishioners, for it happens not here, as it happened to me at Bures, that either the incumbent or his curate, becomes intimately acquainted with his flock individually, but is only in readiness, whenever he hears of sickness, to offer his services, which are mostly declined."[295]

Two days later he wrote home again saying that he had accompanied Mr Norris. "In the course of our walk I enquired in what way it was possible to ascertain when any of the different persons whose houses we passed, were sick, to which he replied that it was impossible and that it would be still more so to me than to him because they would frequently come to him for relief in a pecuniary point of view which they would not do to me! I will follow your advice and in case of nothing presenting itself I will create work. I will, as opportunities occur, make enquiries of the two curates of Gt Hackney in what way they would imagine I should be most contributing to the general good. I am perfectly aware that whatever line is to be pursued it must be begun and continued with great care and discretion . . . "[296]

He then moved into lodgings with a Mrs Nayler in West Street where he asked his mother to send his trunks, "by cheap conveyance as they charged near a pound for luggage by the Companies coach". He described the lodgings: "I have secured some lodgings for which I am to pay forty guineas for the year including washing, cooking and crockery and should I only retain them for six months (which God grant may be the case) twenty five guineas." They were "a short distance from the chapel. There is not such a thing as a nice walk in or about Hackney so that I shall always confine myself to Mr Norris's garden. The bed that I shall occupy is a large four posted one, so that I [am] almost afraid my own sheets will be too small." He wrote home for sheets, table cloths, towels, knife cloths, etc., and finished his letter by sending his love to "my dearest Ellen. She is a dear girl, and I am sure that she will always contribute to my happiness as much which God knows is as much as possible as she does now." He prodded his father impatiently with regard to a Living: "I trust you will not fail in persuading Mr Coleridge to get if possible a promise from a 'certain high person' between this and Christmas."

Johnny was not required to educate the local children as he had been at Bures and his congregation though large, was for the most part 'lower grade'. He found himself socially disadvantaged by being the curate of a chapel rather than a church. He commented on Mr Norris who "appears to me to dwell much more on the necessity of deep theology in a clergyman, as well as Holiness, than upon his performance as a useful and conscientious parish priest."

By August he had settled into his parochial duties and was naturally enjoying life more. He wrote home saying, " My parochial calls at present are but light, as I have only one person in my district, who is anxious of availing herself of any assistance or advice I may be enabled to afford. I am daily making enquiries whether there are any others who would wish me to attend them, but, as yet, I have found none. I have now to take a walk of two miles and a half out and back daily in attending upon a sick person of Mr. Irish's flock, to whom, in the absence of his own minister, I was hastily summoned. He is at the point of Death and is only just sensible. He says that he is quite delighted with me, and never derived so much comfort from any body else's attendance as he does from mine. Mr Irish has given him up into my care. - This last week I have, altogether, had my hands pretty full having taken upon myself a great deal of the Regular Parish Duty, which is at all times very heavy. The Baptisms and funerals are without end, in addition to which there are marriages - duties at the Workhouse and Alms-houses, besides the necessary visitation of the sick. Mr Rennel says that he cannot, by any possibility, get more than two hours a day, (without including meal times) to himself. He has only been in orders since last November, and he conceives that the having the care of such a large and complicated Parish has been of infinite service to him, in a very short time, completely master of the Duties of his profession. - It is wonderful what work both he and Mr. Irish have. I am endeavouring to get them to let me join in the arduous undertaking. - Sunday is my Sacrament Sunday, when Mr. Irish will assist in that Sacred Duty, and has also offered to give me a sermon which I have accepted."[297]

Mr Rennel requested him to become secretary for the Clerical Book Club, which "consists of twelve members, one of which I am to be. It is proposed that I should conduct it's arrangements, because I have the least work in the shape of Parish Duty . . . They intimate to me that if mine was a Church instead of a Chapel I should have the same work as themselves. - I wish I had. - I hope, however, they will not have long to retain me as the secretary of their Book Club which I have undertaken."

Johnny was not fulfilled. His impatient personality came to the fore again and he pressed his father to persuade John Taylor Coleridge to use any connections he might have with the Lord Chancellor. He finished his letter home in August: "I hope, my dear Father, soon to hear that you have had some conversation with Mr Coleridge. Pray do not forget to tell him that I had a large curacy at Bures, where, in addition to a great many sick to attend to I also had a Work-house to superintend as well as Parochial Duty of every kind, besides a school, which I gave a great deal of time to. It may be added also that I had the whole Duty to myself, and that the population of the Parish was from fifteen hundred to two thousand. I moreover got rid of a meeting-house, and always succeeded in having a very full Church every Sunday. - You may tell him too that in my present situation I am endeavouring to avail myself of the opportunities that may be afforded me of becoming still more perfectly acquainted with the Duties of my Profession, by being ready to give any assistance that may be useful in the affairs of the great Hackney Parish : and that I am exacting myself in every way to be of service to the particular individual in my own District. - I hope the Branch Bank is going on perfectly. - I have not yet taken up the five Pounds I threatened I should for my immediate necessities, but having only five shillings in my Pocket I shall be obliged to apply for it early in the coming week. - I am looking forward with hope to a speedy settlement in life. - I am quite well. and comfortable and cheerful. - Give my duty and very dear love to my kind Mother, and Sisters and believe me, My dear Father. Your truly affectionate Son. You may let dear Ellen read this letter."

John Taylor Coleridge had not forgotten Johnny's future. On 1st September he had written to John May saying he was not hopeful of an early meeting with the Bishop. "John however must be moderate and patient."[298]

In November, Mr Norris asked Johnny whether he was interested to have the Duty of St Thomas's Hospital over London Bridge. It was first suggested to him as being worth about £500 a year with a good house, coals and candles. He could also undertake a lectureship at the same time. Johnny made enquiries and found that the offer was not as it perhaps seemed and as ever he leaned upon his father telling him "Now, my dear Father, there is a monstrous deal pro-and-con in the first place the Duty is of the most disagreeable and, I may say, dangerous nature. - the situation I should conceive any thing but healthy - and the calls upon one's time and attention most pressing. - On the other hand, five hundred a year, which I might hold for life, if nothing better offered itself - a comfortable house, and a most respectable situation, are things not to be refused in a hurry. - I fairly own I am afraid of the undertaking.

"No one but those, who have attended at a hospital have any idea of what a man has to undergo in attendance upon the different wards. - the melancholy cases exhibited to his view - and sometimes human nature, in the most deformed and horrid state both of body and mind. The present clergyman of St Thomas Hospital, who is about to give up the duty, said that he had the other day to attend upon a man whose bowels were only resting, almost apart from his body, on the bed; - he was so sick he could scarcely get through his first prayer, and was obliged to leave the poor suffering patient. - Do you think I should have more nerve. - I begin to feel sick at the thoughts of such a sight. But still I aim to get money as I can. . - Such a thing, however, as this could be of little assistance to me, as far as my marriage is concerned - for I should not easily agree, unless it turns out better than I expect, to dear Ellen's if she were inclined, which I am sure she would not be, considering a Hospital over London Bridge as her home, and therefore I could undertake such a duty only with the impression of it's leading to something better. - One thing, for certain, is evident, that Mr Norris is anxious to do something for me, and that I am the first on his list, as I am the only person he has spoken to respecting this affair. Of course, I am placed in a very delicate situation - if I accept the Duty, five hundred a year he may very fairly feel, that he has done a good deal for me. - If I do not accept it - will he offer me any thing else. - Under these circumstances what appears to me to be the best plan, is, that you should immediately write to Mr Norris and explain to him how I am situated with regard to my engagement with dear Ellen, a complete explanation of which, I think, will advise me whether or not to take what he has at present offered." Having shifted the onus upon his father but wishing to stay in Mr Norris's good books he continued, "I cannot sufficiently express to him how grateful to him I am for thinking of me and offering me his services in the kind very kind manner he has. It affords me also no little satisfaction, the perceiving that he feels that he can conscientiously present me as candidate for such a responsible office. It shows at any rate, that he is well pleased at myself.

"I believe, after all, Mr Norris will turn out my sure Patron. Pray my dear Father express to him, in your letter, in the very strongest terms, how grateful I am for his consideration of me, and also add, that I have been most plainly comfortable in my situation as his curate" and "that I should feel very sorry in giving up his curacy for any thing, that would not contribute to hasten my union with dear Ellen. Such you may conscientiously represent as my real feelings, for altho' I do not like Hackney, I would never have such a kind Rector as I at present have, merely because I dislike the place where he resides. - My dear Father a thought has come into my head - cannot you put yourself into a coach - on Friday and come up and stay here till Monday or Tuesday.

"I am sure Mr. Norris will be most happy in seeing you, altho' I believe he cannot give you a bed, as the Bishop of Barbados and his wife will be with him. If you come you can hear the bishop preach a Charity Sermon at the Church in the morning, and your humble servant occupy the same pulpit in the evening, or you may hear me both morning and evening, as I preach in the morning at the Chapel and in the evening at the Church. - I would not however, if you should decide upon a journey, have you delay a moment writing to Mr Norris. He went to Cambridge today and I believe returns on Friday or Thursday. - He gives a dinner

John Taylor Coleridge, 1829, by Mrs Carpenter,

Robert Southey, 1812, after the painting by Sir Thomas Lawrence.

party for the Bishop on Saturday . . . I am going, and at which I am sure he would be most happy in seeing you - but this and the journey you will please yourself about. Pray fail not to express as strongly as possible to Mr Norris, in your letter how grateful I am to him for all his kindness - and give him a whole account of my engagement with dear Ellen. - Do not mention to any one else except Ellen and her family the affair of St Thomas's Hospital, as it is not at present known that the present incumbent is going to leave it - and Mr Norris has several other friends he would wish to see, if I do not wish for it. I shall explore St Thomas's."[299]

    The living was in fact only worth about two thirds of that indicated and he did not feel that it was the sort of home he should offer Ellen. Furthermore it seems that John certainly did not see his future in a London Hospital. He was aware that he would not be penniless in the future and the life of a country parson was no doubt much more appealing to his nature. He deliberated about the post in mental turmoil, very lonely and still immature though now twenty six years old. His father wrote to Mr Norris but the reply, although flattering of Johnny's diligence was perhaps not one that helped him towards the step he felt should be his.

He was also worried regarding his mother's health in Bristol and finally turned upon his friend John Taylor Coleridge again writing to his father in November: "I am beginning a letter to you, but whether I shall have time to finish it for to day's Post, I am very doubtful about. I will, however, in order to loose no time, proceed at once to business. - I perused Mr Norris's letter to you, enclosed for my inspection, in the Bank package. One thing has gratified me exceedingly in it, I mean the manner in which he is pleased to speak of my humble but sincere endeavours to do my Duty, as his Curate. I can conscientiously assert, that, during the five months, I have been resident at Hackney, I have applied myself exclusively to the steady performance of the Duties of my Profession, and should have been content with the answer of a good conscience on this head. I cannot, however, but desire the very greatest pleasure from the reflection that I have not only satisfied my own mind, but have also gained the approbation, and, I believe, regard, of my worthy and good - natured Rector. I set a value upon his praise - because I believe him to be man, who would not, for the sake of flattery, or any other feeling, say, what he did not conceive, in justice ought to be said. I am consequently, as you may imagine, with the notions I entertain of Mr Norris, very highly satisfied with the manner he has thought fit to speak of me in his letter to you. - I am also willing to believe that he will use his best exertions on my behalf, to procure me something, that will enable me to fit in life. I am sure, that were it, at this moment, in his power, to do so, he would be delighted at the opportunity, and I have but little doubt, though he says not a word, that he will not delay to ask any friend of his to assist him in this kind work for my sake.

He last week wrote to the Ld Chancellor, to request a Living for Paroissin, the present clergyman of St Thomas's Hospital. - I hope and trust that he will succeed in doing something for me. - With respect to the Hospital, things are just as they were, but, of course, if Paroissin gets a Living, or even a comfortable curacy, he will immediately give up his present undertaking. - I have had but little conversation with Mr Norris upon the subject, - and when it was brought forward, he only repeated to me, without comment, what he stated in his letter to you. He seems, in that, to consider, that the success of the canvas, supposing it worth while trying for the situation, would in a great measure depend upon your friends. - My own feelings with respect to the affair, are decidedly, as the salary is only £180 - per annum, against my offering myself as a

St Mary's Church, Hale.

candidate. It is true that I may give up the Duty whenever I pleased - but would it be fair upon the Electors, for me (upon not liking the situation, which I am sure I should not,) at once to signify my intention of releasing, when perhaps I only performed the Duties at the Hospital two or three months. - I am sure that I should be perfectly miserable. - God knows my present situation, saving the being under so kind and worthy a Rector, is, uncomfortable enough. - Days and evenings pass away without my having a being to communicate an idea to - and, when I dine out, I seem to be looked upon as inferior to other clergymen, because I am only the curate of a chapel. Even in my own district when Rennel and myself meet at a dinner party, he is requested to say Grace, tho' only ordained a year and a half ago, because he is the curate of the Mother Church. - When I do make the change - I should like to go to a Church, and not a Chapel. - If then such are my feelings at present, what would they be when I was pinned down, on the other side of London Bridge?

"I suppose that my next piece of Preferment, would be, the appointment of Chaplain, to the Prison of Newgate - where I might figure away with Jack Catch. - But joking apart - I do not see the use of my moving from Mr Norris's curacy, till I can get something that enable me to marry. I am willing to rub on even through another six months at the end of which time, the Bishop of Winchester may perhaps, be about to be informed that there is such a person in existence as John May - when he will say he has nothing to give away - I have not yet signified my unwillingness to become a candidate for the Duty at St Thomas's Hospital to Mr Norris. - but if I remain in the same mind, that I am at present in, I will endeavour to do it in as delicate a manner as I can. The truth of the matter is, that, I am afraid to accept the offer, knowing how I should....the Duty - and I am also afraid to refuse it, for fear I should afterwards have to regret such a line of conduct. - If I could be certain of a failure, without having a hand in it, I would become a candidate immediately. - "Hope", it is the scriptures that speak, "deferrel maketh the heart sick" - I had reckoned upon John Coleridge's having exerted himself in some way for me before this time. -

"A year has now nearly elapsed since his friend, (if that person can be called a friend that one is afraid to request a favour of.) has been raised to one of the highest situations in this country, and yet I am, as far as he is concerned as I was before. It appears to me to be an odd thing that John Coleridge should have recommended me to take the Hospital, unless he was in hopes that I should be willing to consider that a sufficient provision for me. - It seems to me to be no excuse that an opportunity has not presented itself of sounding the high personage in question - If I wanted to do something for a friend I would make the opportunity - and if sounding, (an odd term where a friend is the person to be applied to) is necessary - the more need that it should be done quickly. - In writing as I do I may perhaps be too hasty and inconsiderate"

He continued to say that he felt he was exactly in the same situation as six months ago. "But I will say no more. - I will endeavour patiently to await my fate. - I think that the tenor of Mr Norris's letter, leads one to suppose that his notion agrees with mine - that it would be as well that I should not be a candidate for the Duty at the Hospital - I should like to know whether this is your opinion. - He mentions nothing to make one very anxious for it - and I think a great deal to induce one to put a stone upon the matter - I should like to have another letter from you, my Dear Father, upon the subject, as soon as possible - Mr Norris seems to leave the decision entirely to yourself and me. - "My Landlady has requested me to advance her £15 - and I hope therefore it will not be inconvenient for me to draw upon you for £20 . . . £5 myself to morrow - Of course, directly I receive . . .

"It gives me great pain, My dear father to read such bad accounts of my dear Mother - pray in your next letter - give me a full history of her complaint - I shall not be easy till I again hear about her. Give her my very best love, and request her to let me have a letter from herself. - I hope she is at this moment better. - I do not like to hear of Dr Carrick's being called in. - I wish dearest Judy many many happy returns of this day - Give my love to all - and best love to dearest Ellen telling her that I may not perhaps be able to despatch her letter till Wednesday. I shall call upon John Coleridge to morrow and talk about the Hospital." [300]

The attack was most unwarranted. John Taylor continued his efforts to obtain patronage for Johnny both by writing to the bishop and meeting with him. At one stage the bishop expressed the opinion, "that he thought Norris's a bad school for a young clergyman." In July he remarked to John: "At present he is young and has not served a long apprenticeship and things may happen which we don't remotely anticipate now."[301] It seems to be more than a possibility that the bishop wanted to see Johnny behave himself over a good length of time before entrusting him with a living of his own.

Southey wrote to comfort John in December 1828: "God bless you my dear friend, & bring you thro all those difficulties which you had so little reason to expect, & had done nothing to bring upon yourself. The inflictions of injustice are I suppose the most difficult of all evils to bear with equanimity: evils which arise from our own faults we receive as their chastisement & our own deserts, - those which Heaven is pleased to inflict are borne as being its will."[302] By November 1829, John May was reduced to borrowing money from John Taylor Coleridge.[303]

John's brother, William May, had a post in The City in March.[304] Johnny was involved in the scheme for the new King's College, London. This had been officially launched in June 1828, when a Provisional Committee was set up by its secretary, Henry Nelson Coleridge, Sara Coleridge's future husband. Colonel James Coleridge met Johnny in London during January of that year and told John: "I was much pleased to meet your son in London although I was quite unfit for Company the day I dined with him at John Coleridge's - I afterward heard a most excellent account of his good Conduct & Zeal from Mrs Norris who spoke very highly of him." He was concerned about his health and wanting to put his house in order, gently reminded John of a debt and went on to comment regarding the forthcoming family wedding: "I have a return of the numbness in my left arm, which either indicates acid Bile or Angina as my Stomach is often, with me, the seat & cause of my Complaints, it may be the former - or it may be the latter. I hold Physicians rather cheaply, and have heard such contradictory advice from the ablest of them, that my Confidence is destroyed - nay I believe the Exeter Physicians hastened poor George's death - but this Entre Nous - he was more fit for his End, than I am, or ever shall be - for the quiet tenor of his Life, led him in the right path, & he had laboured & done good, & his last years were a preparation for his Journey.

"In my Will Fanny is to have her Share of my little from the Bank Stock I have lent to you, and as there is no notice in the Will of such lending, I am anxious to have it replaced - but I am also anxious that you should not be distressed or put to Inconvenience, by the re transfer; which I hope may not be to your disadvantage. I can only add on this stead, that I am in no hurry about it, if it be done after the next Dividends are paid, it will answer every purpose."

"Henry is bent on marrying his Cousin, which is decidedly against my Judgement - for I set my Face against so near a Connection."[305]

Sara Coleridge married Henry and left Greta Hall in September 1829. "& then we part after six and twenty years residence under the same roof," wrote Southey to John. Sara wrote to John May at Bristol in April, 1830, to express concern at his wife's failing health and also told him how she and Henry had met "Mr John May" at Mr Powles's, a city financier, some months ago and that "We were pleased to hear him so handsomely spoken of in the neighbourhood where he is now residing."[306]

Susanna Frances May died at Clifton on 31st May, 1830. She had been in declining health for over a year. She was buried in the family vault of the Church of St Mary's at Hale on 8th June. In the Chancel is the inscription written by Robert Southey in 1835. The tablet and lettering are estimated to have cost £20. He referred to it and the efforts he was making to finish it, in various letters from July 1833 to 7th November 1835. Then he wrote: "You shall have the inscription as soon as I can produce any thing that does not absolutely displease me; - it has been more often in my mind . . . God bless you my dear old friend, & continue to support you under all difficulties."[307] The inscription reads:-

"In the family vault of this church is deposited all that was mortal of Susanna Frances, wife of John May Esq and the tender mother of four hopeful children, for whom she lived, and in whose arms she died on 31st May 1830 aged 59 years. Her mind was generous, open, sincere. Her manners plain, simple, and noble; Rejecting all sorts of duplicity and disguise as useless to her purpose, and odious to her nature. But her husband inscribes this stone specially to recount her quick and sound sense, cheerful temper, and ardent affection, with which she crowned the happiness of his earlier, and soothed the sorrow of his later years, nor least in all, in gratitude to God for the example of unwavering faith which she was enabled to set before him, in the severe trial of her last long and painful illness, teaching and animating him thereby to bear the heaviest of afflictions in the spirit and the hopes of a Christian."

1830 also marked the death of John's brother Joseph in Versailles on 20th April. He was brought home and buried in the family vault. Since he died intestate Hale Manor passed to his son, also named Joseph. This son was nicknamed 'Wicked Joseph' by the family as his gambling habits were believed to be a contributory factor to the loss of Hale Manor by the family.[308]

In the middle of these sad events John received a letter from John Taylor Coleridge apologising for the intrusion but giving news of a matter of some possible importance to Johnny. "I hear that my old friend Mr Norris is drawing to the end of his earthly pilgrimage; now he holds you know perhaps a good Radnor Living that of Nether Broughton in Leicestershire.This is probably too much for Johnny but the Earl might move another Incumbent and thus free up a smaller benefice. Captain Bouverie's (John May's brother in law) absence from the country makes your mode of approach more difficult and therefore I thought time the more valuable."[309] By February, 1831, Johnny seems to have given up on John Taylor or become occupied with other matters as he asked John May: "Where is John. I never see him and wish I did."[310] In June, John Taylor advised Johnny to find out two or three livings, "at most where the incumbents are likely not to live long and which are about the value which it may be expected Shadwell would have the influence to obtain from Brougham." He suggested one or two including North Fleet in Kent. He pressed Johnny to apply for this living specifically.[311] In October, he was alarmed to receive an uncorroborated report that Johnny had attended a Reform Meeting at Hackney where he had been ill treated. John Taylor considered this quite inappropriate.[312]

On his way home from the West Country, Southey visited John in Bristol, on 17th January, 1831, and discussed his difficulties at the Bank where he was apparently being stabbed in the back both by the Bank itself and his brother William.[313] On 14th March he was lent a further £100 by John Taylor Coleridge and by June it was apparent that not only was he not to get a hoped for uplift in post and income but his position was very much at risk.[314] Having commiserated with John on his harsh treatment by a corporate body acting with no sense or feeling, Southey encouraged him to move north to Keswick, where "the house which is next to ours - standing on the same hill, on the same property, is at this time vacant." "Would to God that you could save enough from the wreck of your fortune to give up all thoughts of any further employment, & take up your abode here in quietness."[315] Through 1831 John attempted to obtain, at first, compensation and later reimbursement for his expenses incurred in setting up the Bank branch.[316]

John experienced the Bristol Reform Bill Riots in 1831 and gave an account to Robert Southey which he, in his turn, passed on to his son in law the Rev J.W. Warter on 27th December, 1831: "You ask me about the insurrection at Bristol . . . A letter from Bristol gives this description, by an eye witness, of what was going on all night in Queen's Square, the main scene of action: 'The mob gave notice of the houses they meant to attack by knocking at the doors, and they allowed the family a quarter of an hour to escape. This interval they spent in dancing: they cleared a circle in the middle of the square, and went round hand in hand, prisoners in their prison dress (drunk with the delight of having been set free) and women of the worst description. The light from the blazing houses made them all appear black; and the dance was to many of them the dance of death, for they were so improvident for their own escape, that they set many rooms and different stories on fire at the same time, and when the roofs fell in many of them were seen to drop into the burning ruins.' It is not known how many perished there, but the number killed and wounded by the soldiers was not short of 500 . . .' The old habit of obedience is destroyed, and what is even worse, there is no longer the bond of mutual interest between the workmen, whether in manufactures or agriculture, and their employers. The poor are poorer than they ought to be; they know this, and they know their own numbers and their strength. Where this is the case, no system that depends upon cheap labour for its prosperity can continue. Great changes in the constitution of our society are therefore inevitable . . ."[317]

Now 56 years old, John's position at the Bank was untenable by the end of 1831. He was unable to continue at the unhealthy, cramped Branch premises situated next to stinking water emanating from the City Poor House with the threat of cholera. Added to this, the riots in which the Bishop's Palace, the Mansion House, some of the prisons and about 100 houses were burnt together with the loss of many lives, made life downright dangerous. Fearing a possible recurrence he suggested that a supply of arms should be stored on the premises as a precautionary measure. The Birmingham Agent was instructed to send six carbines, six sabres, six pikes, one case of pistols, and twelve iron fire buckets to every Branch." [318]

Having received his description of the riots Southey replied to John: "Your escape at the Bank may indeed be deemed providential. Ill as you have been treated by that establishment I should have felt no sorrow for any loss that had befallen it, except so far as the plunder might have enriched the rioters. It is well that nothing was burnt but what money may replace: none of the antiquities of the place. Good God what a scene must that affrighted city have presented."[319] He had told John in October: "You have been most unjustly treated by the Bank, & worse than unjustly by your sister in law & her advisors. And I fear the effect which employment in London might have upon your health." There is then an indication of just how far John's fortunes had swung, "If from the wreck of your fortunes you can get together 300£ a year, with that you might be as well off as the middle order of clergyman, & might live upon it here with perfect respectability & comfort."[320] John finally ceased his employment as the Bank's agent in March 1832.[321]

The Bristol Riots provided employment for John Taylor Coleridge who appeared as one of the Counsel for the Crown. One hundred and two prisoners were tried of whom eighty one were convicted and twenty one acquitted. John wrote to his father 'The Colonel' in January, 1832: "Today has been the day of reckoning; 5 sentenced to execution, and about 18 to transportation for life." His fee was 300 guineas and he was shortly appointed to the Recordership of Exeter and made a Serjeant-at-Law.[322]

John's brother, William, who had been a major contributor to his financial crash in 1822, was once more making life difficult by again attempting to bankrupt him from his position in the City. John Taylor Coleridge wrote in December, 1830: "I must not however close without deeply lamenting all the anxiety Mrs May (William's wife) exposes you to - it is a most ungenerous return for all that you have done. Is it impossible that she may be misled and in ignorance - is there no friend in her confidence who can give her useful impressions."[323] Next February Robert Southey referred John Taylor Coleridge to John May's difficulties with Mrs May and suggested that he see her law advisor paving the way for an arbitration. Southey noted some mention of Arthur Stert's name and a Bond of his which John May held. The dispute apparently arose from the Stert side of the family.[324] In September John signed a loan agreement with John Taylor taking an advance of £350 repayable on demand at 4%.[325] The dispute rumbled on into 1833 when William May was declared bankrupt.[326]

The capital of John's debt of £12,000 incurred in 1821 remained unpaid in February, 1832, and was still a charge upon the estate of Hale.[327]

On the death of his wife Susanna, John inherited her one-third share of Thomas Dea's estate. He also became entitled to a further one-third share left to his wife upon the death of her sister, Charlotte Jane (Dalby) in 1808. By Indentures dated 10th April and 14th May, 1832, the family trust was amended to enable John May to receive the income for his life.[328] His Uncle Thomas Coppendale, who had previously looked after the Lisbon business, died at John's home at Clifton on 4th August, 1833, leaving his estates in Northoram, Halifax, together with his pew in Halifax church, to John in their entirety. Altogether this must have eased his financial plight a little.

John Taylor Coleridge eventually achieved some headway with the Lord Chancellor on Johnny's behalf and Southey encouraged his father in March: "If any one had told me that I should ever feel an anxious interest in any promise of the Lord Chancellor Brougham's, it would have seemed a most improbable supposition, and yet I am now solicitous about two of his promises - that to which you are looking, and that which he made to Henry about the Lunacy Commission . . ." [329]

Young Johnny had ended his engagement to Ellen. He had met Maria Jennings Frampton whilst working in Hackney. She was the daughter of William Frampton of Leadenhall Street.[330] In January, 1833, John Taylor had to advise Johnny May that he knew of complaints that

111

he was neglecting his parochial duties in pursuit of pleasures and thought that this in turn might lead to Mr Norris and Miss Frampton becoming disillusioned. The couple were married by Mr Norris at the Great Church, Hackney, on 17th May, 1834, in the presence of both families. In the same year John's god-daughter, Edith May Southey, married Rev. J.W.Warter . John visited them and kept in touch with his god-daughter for the rest of his life.

Johnny was admitted and instituted as Rector of St Nicholas' Church, Holmpton, East Yorkshire, on 5th March, 1834.[331] His first baptism is recorded on 16th March, 1834, when he proudly signed the register, "John May, Rector."[332] The infant was a baby girl named Ann, daughter of Robert and Ann Froster, farmers. He travelled south again for his wedding. A christening on 18th May was conducted by an officiating minister. The couple then travelled north to begin their new life at Holmpton. The Parish was said to have only 239 people.[333] It was a small windswept, agricultural and seaside parish of approximately 1300 acres and 40 houses. In 1786, the distance between Holmpton Church and the edge of the cliff was 1,200 yards, and in 1833 the distance had reduced to 1,130 yards - 70 yards in 47 years. The church of St. Nicholas is a small Gothic structure, with a chancel, nave, and embattled western tower containing one bell. The tower, which is of brick, was rebuilt in 1832. The church was restored at a cost of £1,000 in 1874, when the walls were cased with brick, red bricks being used for the inside and white for the outside, and the roof raised about 10 feet.[334] The vicarage adjoined the church.

The living had a value of £150 per annum. This concerned both his father and Robert Southey who informed John: "What you tell me of your sons living gives me more concern than surprise, for when you told me that the income arose from the glebe, I was afraid that it must needs partake in the common depreciation of all incomes from the land."[335]

In the south of England the future of Hale Manor was looking increasingly precarious under the stewardship of 'Wicked Joseph' who incurred heavy gambling debts. He had taken loans out on the estate of £3,000 in 1830, £2,000 in 1831, and £4,100 in 1832. He let part of the estate, comprising 2500 acres, to three tenants, one being a Davis Baille. John May's debt of £12,000 together with Joseph's of at least £9,100 were unsustainable and, by 1834, Hale Manor was mortgaged to James Maxse for £29,000 on the security of the estate at 4% p.a.[336] By this date

Joseph had left England for Ireland. A Receiver was appointed for James Maxse on June 27th, 1834, and two farms were transferred to him out of the estate. The Estate was finally sold out of the family to Joseph Goff on 22nd July, 1836.

John May continued to live at Clifton whilst looking for an appointment and was forced to sell part of his treasured collection of books.[337] He saw a good deal of Southey's old friend Cottle and his sister and they spent Christmas with him. John considered working for the new Poor Commission but this does not seem to have materialised. In his offers of help in the summer of 1834 Southey also cautions care: "because it seems to me very doubtful whether the system will be proceeded in & not unlikely that, if it is, the travelling commissioners may be exposed to some personal danger.[338,339]

Samuel Taylor Coleridge died at Highgate on 25th July, 1834, leaving his estate to his wife Sara.

In spring of the following year, Southey left his son in Sussex with his daughter while he moved his sick wife, Edith, back home to Keswick from York. He confided in John: "The far greater number of incurable patients in the asylum are kept there that they may be out of the way of their respective families, though they are perfectly harmless. This may be necessary in some cases, but where it is not necessary it seems to me that we are no more justified in thus ridding ourselves of a painful duty than we should be in sending a wife or a mother to die in an infirmary, that we might escape the pain and trouble of attending upon a death-bed."[340]

John Taylor Coleridge was raised to the Bench in January 1935 and his father, 'the Colonel', attended the Assizes on the Western Circuit that summer.

Johnny and Maria started their family at Holmpton. Their daughter was born on 10 April, 1835, and baptised Maria Charlotte by her father on 10th May. Southey was quick to congratulate the new grandfather and invite him to Keswick, again reminding him: "Tthere is a coach from York to Penrith, so that I may hope one day to see you here, as well as in town."[341] The proud grandfather made the trip to Holmpton in July that year.[342] No doubt he and his son discussed his plans for leaving Clifton with his daughters. He made the move he made later in the year, taking his family to Blackheath. By so doing he was able to raise capital and then rent accommodation at his new venue. After he returned home

John travelled to Tarring in Sussex to see his goddaughter.[343]

Maria gave birth to a baby son on 17 April 1837, baptised John Coleridge Frampton by Johnny at Holmpton on 5th July. John was the family name, Coleridge reflected the close connections enjoyed by both John Mays with that family, and Frampton was Maria's maiden name.

In Blackheath John May formalised his family arrangements by taking a tenancy of 8 St Germans Terrace, one of twelve houses built in the mid 1820s known as the 'Tea Caddy' houses.[344] He was to remain at this address with three daughters and three servants until his death in 1856. The tenancy was then taken by his daughter Miss Susanna Louisa May. He was still involved with the Insurance business. In August Robert Southey asked him for advice concerning a new policy and the likely bonus.[345] Edith Southey died on 16th November. In May 1839, when he returned from a journey to the continent, Southey announced to John his intention of marrying Caroline Bowles, his friend of many years.[346] The marriage took place on 4th June at Boldre Church in the New Forest. (Boldre was once the living of the Rev. William Gilpin known for his 'Picturesque Tour' to the lakes of Cumberland and Westmoreland.) The marriage split the family. Apparently neither John nor his goddaughter, Edith, were able to attend the ceremony even though Southey had told John how much he looked forward to introducing him to his wife.[347] On his way home to Keswick, Southey passed a few days in London seeing his old friend for the last time. The Warters supported Caroline's position and she maintained a correspondence with John from 1839 until at least 1846, three years after Robert's death on 21st March, 1843.[348] His funeral took place at Crosthwaite Church, Keswick, on a stormy day. His son Cuthbert recounts that: "His only intimate friend within reach, Mr Wordsworth, crossed the hills that wild morning to be present."[349]

The May family re-geared their finances and further amended the John Dea Will Trust on 13th April, 1843. They arranged for John to enjoy the "Dividends interest and annual proceeds " of his four children's share of Thomas Dea's estate for life and provided that one quarter of the estate was to be transferred to Rev. John May upon his father's death.[350] John was then 72 and his son 41. Francis Almeric, Lord Churchill undertook to execute a Mortgage Bond for his son with John in the sum of £5,000 with interest.[351]

Life carried on at Holmpton where Johnny remained the vicar until

Tea Caddy Houses, St Germans Terrace, Blackheath.
By courtesy of The Greenwich Heritage Centre.

1845. He had applied for an exchange of living to Gloucester in November, 1838, but was not successful. His work was rewarded with the responsibility of a larger agricultural parish at Ugborough, in Devon. George May Coleridge, at St Mary Church, Torquay, wrote to his godfather, John May, thanking him for obtaining a place for William at Greenwich Naval School and continued: "I must also heartily congratulate you in John's appointment to the living of Ugborough which I see is 20£ in the Kings books and I should hope will improve his income considerably as well as tend to improve his wife's health - It is near the moor and I should say a very healthy spot & I trust both of them may live long to enjoy it . . . I should be sure to fall in with the Vicar of Ugboro' . . . once a year, if not oftener, & shall have no doubt that we shall also become better acquainted by neighbourly visits one with the other. - Let us hope that we shall have the pleasure of seeing you once more in the fair County of Devon & in its' fairest portion of South Hams. - Your brother William will be very near, of whom I have been purchasing lately some Vin Ordinaire."[352]

The Exeter Flying Post reported the arrival on 4th September, 1845, - "John May B.A. - Was instituted to the Vicarage of Ugborough, Devon, void by the death of John Spry, on the Presentation of the Wardens and Commonalty of the Mystery of Grocers, of the City of London."

William White's History, Gazetteer, and Directory of Devonshire - 1850 recorded the Living in the following way: "The vicarage, valued in K.B. at £20 and in 1831 at £260, is in the patronage of the Grocer's Company, London, and incumbency of Rev. John May, B.A., who has a good residence, and 70A. of glebe. The rectorial tithes were appropriated to Plympton Priory. In 1768 Cphr. Savery, Esq., sold nearly the whole of these tithes to the principal landowners, and the remainder, with the advowson, to the Grocer's Company. By a commutation in 1842, the vicar has £185, and Sir W. P. Carew £202 yearly, in lieu of tithes."

The family moved to Ugborough where two daughters were born, Susanna Frances on 28th April, 1847, and Alice Kitson on 6th November, 1849. Johnny baptised both little girls. In the 1851 census the family, with the exception of John Coleridge, who was probably at school, are all recorded at the Vicarage together with a Governess, a Nurse, a Cook and a Housemaid. The vicarage, now owned by the National Trust, is situated at the foot of Parson's Lane to the south of the church and stands in nearly four acres of land. Tradition has it that the vicarage was built around 1555. Certainly it has early Georgian features and has been extended in Victorian times. John May's predecessor, John Spry was instituted as Vicar on 5th March, 1810. During his incumbency he made many improvements to the Vicarage house and gardens. The pond was filled in and a walled garden made on the side. A bridge was built over the stream and a drive carried over it to the house. The garden was laid out and many trees planted and "the whole property greatly improved." The gardens are still a beautiful feature, the stream flowing under the small bridge and it is nice to imagine Johnny and his family enjoying them after the bleakness of their Yorkshire living. In 1846 the Grocers Company spent £250 on improving the vicarage.[353]

Johnny's time at Ugborough was full of interest and activity. New steps were built from the 'Town Place' or village square to the North of the church in 1848. These encroached on manorial waste, the property of The Lord and a case went to court. The result was that Dame Elizabeth Carew and Sir Walter Carew permitted the steps and John May and the church officials signed that the freehold of the 'Town Place' of Ugborough vested in the Lord of the Manor. After the case was settled a Lych gate was erected in 1857 at a cost of £42-10-0. During 1861 and

1862 re-seating and building of the South Transept together with extensive restoration of the inside of church was carried out. The Sanctuary and Chancel were redecorated and large windows constructed on the north and south side of the aisle. At the same time Johnny presented the church with a new font."[354] Further restoration took place in 1867 and in 1868 an organ was installed.

John May (the elder) spent his latter years on various committees including the Select Committee of the Blackheath District of the Society for Promoting Christian Knowledge, The Governors of Magdalen Hospital and the Board of Guardians of Lewisham Union.[355] He suffered from gout and bad eyesight..

The family were outraged on 26th October, 1850, when Johnny's sister, Mary Charlotte, aged 47, married a Samuel Newberry of Shoreditch at the Parish Church. Her residence at the time of marriage is also stated on the marriage certificate as being "Shoreditch". Neither of the John Mays were present at the ceremony and the wedding was conducted by the local curate. In the utmost distress John wrote to his father from Devon three days later: "My beloved and afflicted Father. Bitter, bitter indeed has been the intelligence which this day's Post has brought me. - I can not yet realize the sad event to my mind. I can not cease to love the sister who, though not to the full extent, yet by leaving her father's house as she has done, too truly thereby has forsaken the guide of her youth and has forgotten the covenant of her God. - May, My sadly distressed parent, - the affectionate Father's forgiveness on Earth be satisfied by "Our Father which is in Heaven," and though distress, and anguish, - bitter lamentation with, - perhaps, - unavailing remorse, as the consequence of her conduct, may be the self-elected lot of her remaining days, - yet, I fervently pray, that, for Jesus Christ's, my still beloved sister may be supported in the degradation which now alas! too clearly is awaiting her. - I fervently pray, - my dearest Father. - that, a gracious and an understanding providence will support yourself, and my two dear sisters in this bitter affliction and heavy visitation. - I now, at once, proceed to make a proposal which Maria and I think best calculated to alleviate part of the painful recollections, which must for ever press upon you. - Every meal you take, - every walk, - every association with home must be connected with her we have lost. - Will you therefore with Susan and Charlotte come and spend some months with us, spend the winter with us. I make this unlimited invitation because while you three will occupy our House we shall wish to have no one else, - and, that you may not consider yourself under an obligation to us. -

"I will at once say, - (for you know Dear Father, - that I cannot afford to increase my family for an unlimited time) that, we can easily make an arrangement which will indemnify us, - and be very easy to you. - This I merely add to show you that, - we are not rashly offering what we would not be justified in doing. - Earnestly would I recommend you forthwith to let your House. - Come down here, and, - at your leisure, concoct a plan for a departure from Blackheath, - a continuance at which, - (as it appears to my mind,) must henceforth lie accompanied by sad associations, - calculated to keep open a wound, - which, - I pray God, - My beloved Parent, - may not hasten the end of your valuable life, bringing down your grey hair with unusual 'sorrow to the grave'.

Rev Johnny May's Font, Ugborough

"I will only add that the offer which is now made, - is both by myself and my dear wife made with the utmost sincerity of Heart. - That God in Heaven may, - at this trying moment, - bless, - preserve and keep, yourself, and my two dear Sisters, Susan and Charlotte, - mercifully forgiving her whose name I do not know, - in the fervent prayer Dear Father, Your Dutiful and Affectionate Son.

               "John May"[356]

It is difficult now for us to realise the scandal that was caused by an elder daughter deserting her family, leaving her home for that of her lover, and abdicating her responsibilities to her aged father for an unsuitable marriage. Her happiness was very short lived. In 1851 Mary Charlotte Newberry was again living at 8 St German's Terrace,

Blackheath, with no mention of her husband who was perhaps detained elsewhere! Her father, completing the census return omitted the word 'Lady' against her name unlike her sisters who were given that title. In his distress he entered her age as 37!

Mary seems to have left John's home or moved back to Samuel temporarily as she wrote to her father pleading for money on his behalf: "My most beloved father this is my beloved Samuel's sentiment and he hopes you will not be displeased at my writing it for him, he would have been too long." Apparently Samuel was only partly literate or terrified of John. He admitted owing two sums of money, £4-10s and £14 and assured John that this was the whole sum of his debts. He went on to say he would never rest until "I have been successful in obtaining some employment". He grovelled in begging forgiveness and promised "to act better in future and avoid all bad company." It seems that John was not prepared to write to his daughter. Mary's sister, probably Susanna, wrote to her the same day, giving her father's reaction and a cheque for £14 to take to Samuel the next day, which he could cash at the bank. With regard to the £4-10s, John decided that this was not urgent and although he would help if necessary he trusted that by next April Samuel would have "proved the sincerity of the promises he now makes with regard to his conduct and obtained some respectable employment and if he does act up to all that he expresses to do in his letter to Papa it will tend greatly to help to improve Papa's feelings towards him".[357]

Relationships did not improve with Samuel and John's last will and testament together with a codicil dated 6th February, 1856, excluded Mary Charlotte and gave two fourth parts of his estate to Susanna Louisa May and one fourth part each to John May and Charlotte Livius May. The will was a device advised by Edward Whitaker, John's solicitor, to ensure that Samuel Newberry did not get his hands on any of the family estate.[358] John, always loyal to his family, intended that Susanna act 'In Loco Parentis' for Mary Charlotte should she need her share in the future. He told Susan: "You already know my reason for bequeathing you a double share of my property and omitting altogether from my Will the name of your elder sister."[359]

Susanna, then head of the household, omitted any description of Rank for Mary Charlotte when she completed the 1861 Census return.

John May died at 8 St German's Terrace on Tuesday, 6th May, 1856, in the presence of Sarah Cottle, his and Robert Southey's great friend. He was buried alongside his wife in the May family vault at the Church of St Mary, Hale. It contains the coffins of his grandmother, grandfather by marriage, his father and mother, and most of his brothers and sisters. The pulpit is placed over the entrance to the vault, in the South Transept and it occupies the whole of the Transept extending to within about 1ft of the base of the Archer Monument. The vault was built around 1790 and the first person to be buried in it was Mary Sherman. She is supposed to have been a Governess to the Miss Mays, but it is probable that she was a lady with connections to the Lisbon days of the Sherman and Coppendale families. John May was the last of the family to be buried in the vault.

On the North West side of the Chancel there is a tablet with the inscription :-

"In memory of John May, an English Merchant of unspotted integrity, a man full of charity - a Christian of unclouded faith. He was tried in many sorrows - but supported in all, and died in a good old age leaving four children to mourn his loss and by God's help to walk after his example.

        He was born   Jan 26th 1775.
        And died   May 26th 1856
        Not dead but sleepeth. St Matt. IX. 24"

John's son showed the Christian compassion of his calling by including all his sisters in the memorial.

The remnants of John's library came up to auction on 10th August, 1856, described as "The Library of the Late John May, Esq of Blackheath". The library comprised 517 books and included works owned, written and signed by Robert Southey and members of the Coleridge family. Also at Lot 203 a title that was close to John's heart - "Thucydides, History of the Grecian War, translated by Hobbes, 2 vol in 1, 1812."

By 1861 Johnny May was 59 and approaching the end of his career. He had inherited money by his grandfather's as well as his father's wills and still lived at the vicarage in Ugborough with his wife Maria, two daughters, Susanna Frances and Alice Kitson, a Governess, a Cook, a Housemaid, a Child's Maid and a Lady's Maid. He retired in 1869 at the age of 67 and with his family moved his home to Woodside, Earley, near Reading. The new Incumbent at Ugborough was the Rev. John Frederick Fixsen, M. A., who, in 1859, had married Annette Brakspear of the

Henley on Thames brewing family.

On 10th July 1873 Johnny officiated at the wedding of his son, John Coleridge, to Ethel Mary Scaife and, on 1st April, 1874, his first grandson, John Cyril May, was born. John Coleridge followed in his grandfather's footsteps and joined the Equitable Insurance Company where he worked for forty years, resigned in 1901, and purchased Curvalion House, Creech St Michael, Somerset in 1902.

Annette Fixsen died. On 23rd May, 1878, Johnny again officiated at a family wedding, this time that of his daughter, Alice Kitson, who married the Rev. John Fixsen at Earley Parish Church. So Alice, to whom Johnny gave his Journal of a Short Tour to the Lakes and on which her name is also written in her hand, returned to Ugborough, this time as the vicar's wife. She had a ready-made family of a stepson, aged 14, and a stepdaughter aged 10. She and John then had four children born at Ugborough between 1880 and 1884. They were baptised by John Fixsen at Ugborough. In 1885, Alice and her family left Ugborough for Bucknell Entire Parish in Shropshire where she had three more children. She was still living there at the turn of the new century.

John Coleridge May and his pregnant wife, Ethel, visited his father at Earley towards the close of 1878. On 24th December, 1878, Johnny's third grandchild, Margaret Noel, was born there. As one light is lit another is extinguished. Johnny's health had been deteriorating and on 27th May 1879 he passed away at Woodside aged 77. He was buried at Earley St Peter Parish Church on 3rd June.

His widow Maria spent her days with her family. She visited Alice Kitson at Ugborough in 1881, John Coleridge at Hope Park, Bromley and Susanna Frances at Sunnyside, Reading. Susanna was with her when she died, aged 90, on 10th March, 1897. Johnny and Maria's first born daughter, Maria died in Devon in 1858; their son John Coleridge in Somerset in 1902; and Susanna Frances in 1935 at Reading, a spinster aged 88.

Before she died Susanna Frances May made application to the College of Arms for "Armorial Bearings to be borne and used by her and the other descendants of her grandfather 'the said John May deceased'". Her request was granted in 1913.[360]

Aunt Charlotte Livius May had married Thomas Smallpiece in 1864. The family arranged a settlement on her behalf on 11th April.[361] Johnny's other Aunt, Susanna Louisa, remained at 8 St German's Terrace,

Blackheath, renamed 16, Shooters Hill, until she died at home on 23rd February, 1885. His daughter, Susanna Frances, then still living at Woodside, Earley, was present at her death.

Johnny had two grandsons. John Cyril May had one child by his first wife, a son christened John Maunsell Frampton May. He died of a disease contracted abroad and without issue. The second grandson was Arthur De Kewer Livins May who had six daughters. The direct male line of the John Mays of Richmond thus died out.

The May Family Crest.
Opposite: The front cover of the bound Journal of a Short Tour to the Lakes

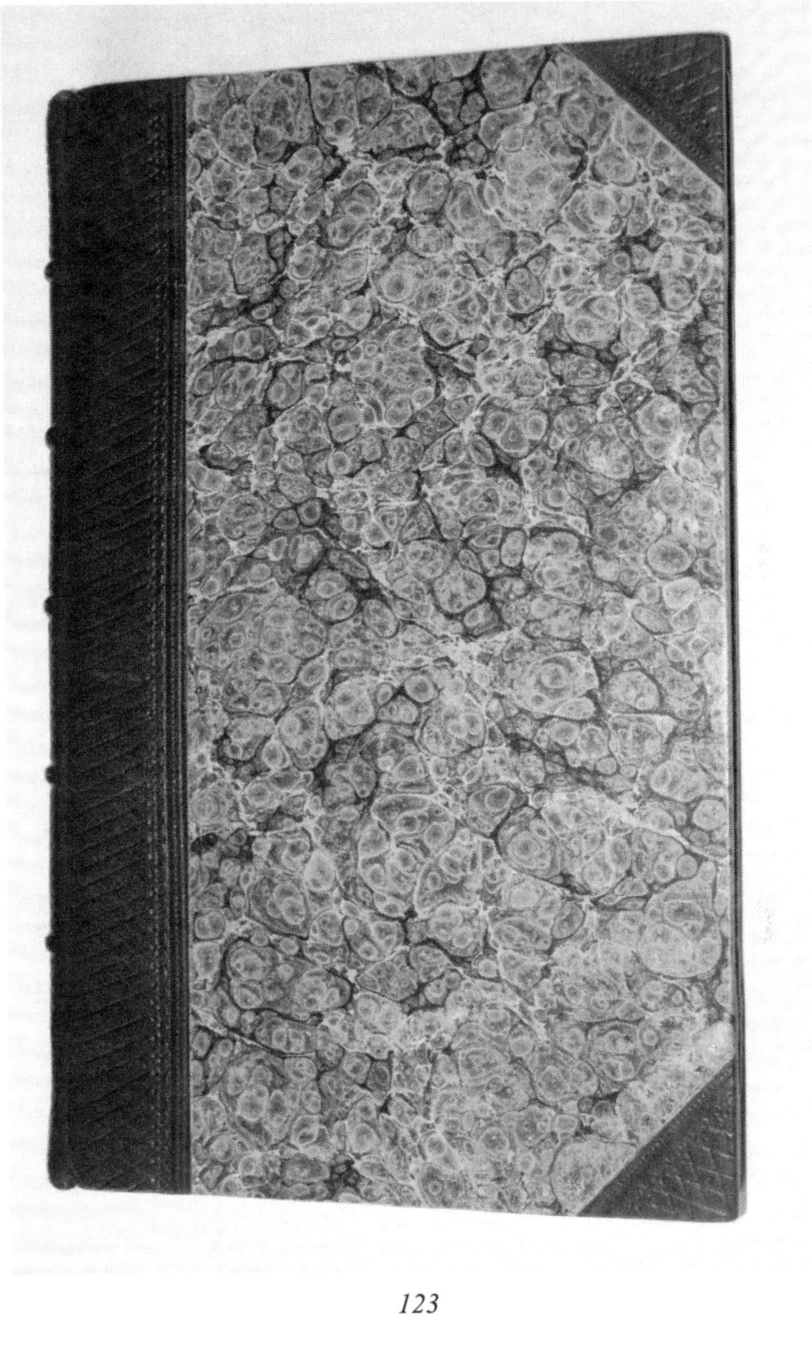

*Above: View from Richmond Hill taken from next to The Wick.
Below: St. Nicholas Church, Holmpton*

"The Journal of a short tour to the Lakes of England: begun from July 29th 1822."

After having, for a long time, looked forward to an expedition as far as "the Lakes" with my father; but, owing to circumstances, having been put off from week to week, I had, at last, the moment of starting, which is on "Monday the 29th of July. 1822."

The circumstances of my having had to reside for about six weeks in London, previous to my journey, will cause me to experience greater pleasure in viewing the most delightful scenery, than I should, otherwise, have felt, had I proceeded immediately from a beautiful spot.

I have never taken any great pleasure in a London life, but least of all, in the "Summer", when you are made most completely to feel what you miss in the country, by the confinement you necessarily meet with in town.

Although, indeed, there are some, who will endeavour to persuade you "that the enjoyments of a London life surpass those of a country" yet, I think, I shall never be able to convince myself "that the walking up and down Bond St. is, in any degree, preferable to the fine air you experience on Richmond Terrace: — nor, do I conceive that, when I return from my little tour, I shall prefer the fine mountains in Hyde Park to the flat campaign country of

125

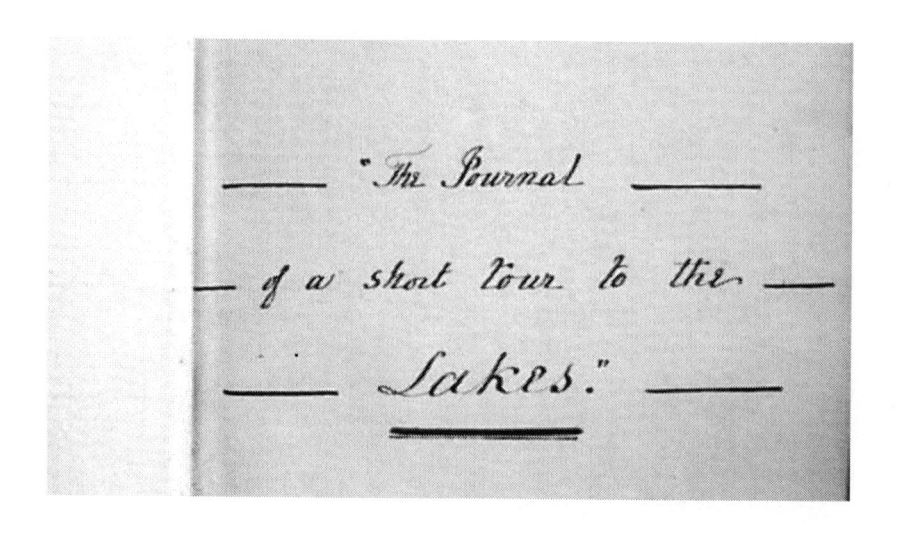

The Journal of a short tour to the Lakes
John May
July 27 th, 1822

The Journal of a short tour to the lakes of England; begun from July 29 th, 1822:.-

After having, for long time, looked forward to an Expedition as far as "the Lakes" with my father; but, owing to circumstances, having been put off from week to week, I hail, at last, the moment of starting, which is on "Monday the 29th of July., 1822."

The circumstances of my having had to reside for about Six weeks in London previous to my journey, will cause me to experience greater pleasure in viewing the most delightful scenery, than I should, otherwise, have felt, had I proceeded immediately from a beautiful spot.

I have never taken any great pleasure in a London life, but

least of all, in the "Summer", when you are made most completely to feel what you miss in the country, by the confinement you necessarily meet within town

Although, indeed, there are some, who will endeavour to persuade you " that the enjoyments of a London life surpass those of a country " yet, I think, I shall never be able to convince myself " that the walking up and down. Bond St is, in any degree, preferable to the fine air you experience on Richmond terrace : - nor, do I conclude, that, when I return from my little tour, I shall prefer the fine mountains in Hyde Park to the flat campaign country of * Cumberland . . . or the fine lake of the Serpentine to the little pool of Keswick. ………………………………….Let not these remarks, however, be considered as prejudice, - for no Englishman will ever be able justly to cry down his own Metropolis - and that the Metropolis of the World - but they are only intended to intimate what the feelings of the writer are with regard to the comparison of "Town and Country." …………… …… …………… Once more, then. - Let those, who stand up for a "London", in

*I do not mean to say that it is impossible to rise early in London - for that would be absurd - but I do mean to say "that as long as fashionable society keep the late hours they do, at present, - it will be more healthy to encroach upon morning with our rest, than to debar ourselves of the proper quantum: - altho' this, even will not be so healthy, as "rising early and going to rest early."

---

*Sweet is the calm that rural scenes impart,
To guide the thought, and purify the heart;
'Tis not in busy towns that nature reigns,
Her home is in the woods, the hills, the plains;
Not in the eager crowd, but in the fields
The quickening soul it's free born homage yields;
Nor' midst the schemes of man it's powers expand,
But in the works of an Almighty hand;
Where the minutest seed, the leaf, the flower,
Proclaims the wonders of it's author's power.

No longer here, by worldly ties confined,
We cramp and curb, by fashion's laws, the mind;
But breathing unconstrained and freer air,
To serve JEHOVA in his courts prepare.
It's sacred duties on the heart imprest,
Here Sunday shines a day of general rest.
Throng'd is the well-known way so often trod,
"The village foot-path to the house of GOD".
———————————*
"Oh! Friendly to the best pursuits of Man,
Friendly to thought, to virtue, and to peace, -
Domestic life in Rural- pleasure pass'd ! "

Cowper

*The comment and Cowper's poem above are written on the opposing leaves to pages 3 and 4 of the Journal which is otherwise left blank.

opposition to a "Country," life, consider whether the enjoyments of the one are not more conducive, in general, to "Health" - that blessing of life - than the en= = joyments of the other. - Which is the most healthy - * (see opposite page) *the rising early and going to bed early - or the rising late and going to bed late? - Which of these contributes to show off the beauty, and improve the health of the fair sex ? - Is it not more delightful to witness the pretty merry girl, after a good nights' rest, come down early, on a Spring morning - dressed neatly but not gaudily - and with blooming cheeks, ready for a walk before breakfast; - than to see the fine handsome lady of town, decked out and breakfasting at"one" o clock - with complaints of headache and worn out looks ? - Then - with regard to Men - Which is most manly, and contributive to their health - the rising at "five" in the morning - dressed in "tough shooting clothes - with their gun on their shoulder, - and accompanied with their faithful dogs - to hunt the country for Game? - or to find them just arrived in Bond St from breakfast at "12" o clock - dressed in superfine cloth - With a Switch in their hand - walking in search of finding admirers ? -Then - again - in a higher point of view -** (see opposite page) *On a Sunday morning - which is most pleasing ? - to see the streets interspersed with fops, preparing to idle away the whole day - and consume its' precious moments in folly if not in wickedness? - or - when the bell is sending it's melody across the quiet fields, - to behold the peasantry in their best finery, with ruddy faces and modest cheerfulness, thronging tranquilly along the green lanes to Church - and, when that holy day is drawing to a close, to see them in the evenings, gathering about their cottage doors, and appearing to exult in the humble comforts and embellishments, which their own hands have spread around them? - It is this sweet home-feeling - this settled* repose of affection in the domestic scene, that is, after all, the parent of the * steadiest virtues and purest enjoyments . . . . . .

Many other things might be brought forward in favour of a "country life", but as that is not the object of my little book, I will abstain from any more comparison, at present; - letting what I have said suffice to show with what delight I quit "LONDON" for the "COUNTRY."

However, before I am obliged to begin upon my "Journal", I must make one more observation . . . In a "Tour" especially a young man's, all depends upon his companion: - and - when a visit is in the course of it - the character of his host _____ Now the prospect, in this respect, that I have to look forward to, is most rich - in the one case as well as the other. - My companion is my father - than whom I could not have - or - if I could - should not wish - a better. - And - when I recollect that it is principally - indeed I may say - wholly, on my account that he makes this tour (for - as he himself has stated, - there are essential reasons, which would, otherwise, deter him) it cannot but excite in my mind that gratitude, which, laying aside my duties and feelings as a Son to a father, would naturally arise towards a friend, and one, who takes every opportunity of gratifying me . . . . It is "with truth", and, I hope, a right adequate feeling, - that I aver - independently of having acted towards me, as the kindest and best of fathers would towards the best and most meritorious of Sons - (a title, which, I am ashamed to say, I cannot, in any degree, bear - having, too often, frustrated him in what he expected from me - but - still, with God's help and assistance, determining, I trust, before it is too late, to make up for those faults I have committed - and those opportunities I have missed of improving myself, - and gratifying him already too indulgent to me) - independent of

The Wick, Richmond circa 1826

this - he has always wished to make me his companion, - and has treated me as his bosom friend; - not neglecting to administer those useful admonitions and instructions to me, that devolved upon him, as my father. -

This, then, is my companion: - and - the persons, whom I am going to visit, are my father's most intimate friends; - as a most worthy family: - the head of which has distinguished himself to the world, by the memorous and most excellent publications - in prose and poetry - that have come out in his name. - the perusal of any of which, will convince the reader that the author is one of the - most learned - most entertaining - and most excellent of men. ____ So that what with my companion - and my host - I may safely say, "that I go to the "Lakes" with as good prospects of gaining instruc=tion and pleasure (if duly appreciated & sought after, on my part) as any who have preceded me.

"The Journal"

On Monday July 29th my father and I started from Tavistock St at 5 o clock in the morning, to meet the Birmingham coach, by name Crown - Prince, at the Belle - Savage Inn Ludgate-hill, from whence we proceeded a little before the half hour: and after passing through a fine, open, and beautiful country, as well having past thro' St Albans, a clean but narrow - old looking town, containing a most handsome Abbey - Church, which appears at some distance before you reach the town itself, - we arrived at "Redburn", our fourth stage, where we breakfasted, and afterwards commenced our journey, still passing through the most delightful scenery - witnessing the fields rich with harvest, and covered with reapers and gleaners till we got beyond "Dunstable", where the country began to appear flatter and less rich, than we had found it in Hertford-Shire, Bedford= Shire and Bucks both being more flat and less interesting : so that from "Dunstable" to a little before you come to "Weedon" the country does not require much notice:- but on the righthand-side of the road as you approach this last place, a small church with a fine house and some cottages presents a very pretty view, and at no great distance from hence, on the other side of Weedon, and the same side of the road, there is another similar object, the adjacent country still continuing to be very beautiful. - About 4 miles distant is "Daventree" a small and narrow town, as far as I could judge of it, (but it was then raining very hard) and here we turned off the Mail-road, which leads to "Coventry" and journeyed on to "Southam", where we dined:- but the country, the whole way from Daventree, is most attractive; - the richness of the foliage - the verdant aspect of the meadows - and the

Ludgate Hill

pleasing sight of the corn-fields, mostly cut, could not afford, any-where, greater delight to the eye than they did here: - the country that we had already seen was very beautiful - but here it was still more. - in some parts it was extensive, espcially as you approach close to Southam - and in others meadow - ground, within a narrow compass, the track, which we were travelling resembling more that of a lane, than that of a turnpike road. - But the delightful country did not end here, for, altho' for a short distance from Southam, it does not attract the attention so much, yet, upon the approach to "Leamington" it renews it's beauty in still greater perfection than it did even before; and a little before you enter that place, on the right hand side, the view of a house very prettily situated in the midst of very fine timber foliage, and meadow - ground, not excepting the corn-fields affords a fine sight from the road; - and Leamington itself - rather a gay-place, is very delightfully situated ; - but, however upon our approach to "Warwick" I was beyond measure delighted. === At some distance before you enter this place, you have a view of St Mary's church - tower and the Castle, which only prepares you for what you have to witness, when you come nearer : - for - as you approach, the bridge with a nearer view of the castle and church opens itself to your sight ; - and is very fine - but when you are actually upon it - , the sight of the Castle is far more impressive : - You look down upon the Avon, and see, on it's banks the finest stone - building, I can conceive, any one would wish to see : - the walls are very lofty - and taking up a great space in length : - but this is not all - you see, in the midst of fine rich trees, the towers of this beautiful building - not, indeed, the whole of them, but, what is considerably better, their tops surmounting the trees : - and the water immediately below the walls has a most enchanting effect, adding considerably to the scenery. = The town of Warwick is large and clean : - as you enter you have, on your right-hand, a view of a small - church, and a little further on the same side, a sight of St Mary's a fine hand = = some - building, passing by, on your left, the Town - hall, which is a stone building - then - when you turn off, opposite the Warwick Arms pass under an iron - bridge, and close to the walls of the jail, which are very high ; - and at some distance further the Gas-works : - the whole, from the Castle to where our Coach went out, affording a very interesting passage. Indeed the view of the Castle was the most beautiful thing I had ever seen - and surpassing all my imagination about it, which was, by no means, small.

    From Warwick we proceeded on, passing through interesting country, for 20 miles, till, (a quarter before eight) we arrived at Birmingham, - the entrance to which is rather-striking - and the town itself a complete second - but inferior

Warwick Castle

London. - When we entered we found it in the highest state of confusion, owing to the wakes, which were then going forward, - and, I presume, in some degree, to the celebrated Mr Wooller and Cobbett, who had, only very lately, been released from Warwick jail : - as soon, however as we arrived at the Inn the Coach puts up at, we went in search of our Hotel, which is called "the Royal Hotel", where we made preparations for the night; and then took a little stroll as far as the Theatre, returned, supped, went to bed, and partook of a most delightful night's rest. = Upon the whole we had a very pleasant journey, altho' the rain descended very plentifully at times, but being well equipped for the purpose we did not experience much discomfort, but only had to regret that it somewhat interfered with the beautiful aspect of the country. - Thus ended the day of our journey =

On Tuesday, the 30th, immediately after breakfast we walked about Birmingham, and saw Lord Nelson's statue, which is very handsome: and, happening to go into a cutler's shop to buy a razor-strop, we were shown a knife, which was made at Sheffield - containing 400 blades - only 4 inches long - consisting of 5000 parts - and costing 200 guineas - without exception the most curious and ingenious thing I ever saw. - We then proceeded on to Mr Boulton's.- But, before I go further I must say-that the whole appearance of Birmingham is most uninteresting - no fine buildings - no shops remarkable for their outside appearance, and show - in every thing looking dirty - and the people appearing, what, indeed, I believe they are, the dirtiest and most profligate of Mankind. - Soho was our next object - It is about 2 miles distant from Birmingham, and part of it in Stafford-shire, - the residence of Mr Boulton is very pleasant and secluded - altho' close to the Turnpike road. - After going though his grounds we went to see part of his manufactory, and saw the whole process of the "Mint" - and what wonderful power steam has, being, as Mr Boulton himself stated, equal to the power, which was required at his manufactory, to eleven horses, working together : - besides this, which is most curious and too hard for me to describe, Mr Boulton showed us many other things, all at the manufactory, which is the largest in the world. =

We, then, went, under the guidance of Mr Robinson, to whom Mr B. introduced us, to visit the Pin manufactory, which delighted me more than the one I had just quitted. We saw the state of the wire, as brought into the manufactory, and then witnessed how it was brought to proper thickness of Pins, which is effected by means of drawing it through a steel hole of the size of a regular Pin, thus lengthening and making more of the wire itself. besides gaining the other point : - it was, then, taken

Matthew Boulton's manufactory at Soho

off the roller, which was used in drawing it, and we were shown how it was made straight, by pulling it between steel pegs, placed quite even and close together, so that nothing, but the wire itself could go between,- and - , then, being drawn through these pegs, nearly the whole length of the room, by the little boy appointed for that purpose, - the quantity, so drawn, was quite straight. the next process, then, to be seen, was a great many of these straight wires cut into a length, so that out of each six pins could be made; - we then saw how these were sharpened, being, first made quite rough and afterwards quite smooth, simply by means of two wheels, of different quality ; - the same man, then, showed us how they were cut into the proper length for Pins, after which we went into another part of the manufactory to see how the brass was made white, but, owing to the workmen not being there, it was only faintly described, we, however, saw the women put them into the papers, as they are sold - which is most curious - for they have an iron thing fixed upon a table, with little grooves along it, the size of the Pins, and at the same distance from one another as you see the Pins in the paper : - this iron is so constructed, that it opens so as to let two or three rows of paper, folded up, be put in, which is placed beyond the grooves - the women, then, put the pins into the

Inside the Manufactory

grooves, and, with a leather safe guard for their thumbs, push them through the paper - they, then, take the whole out of the machine, and pull down the paper which was folded up without any pins, but now having them all in, - and you see them in the paper as you buy them - we, then, saw how the heads were put on; which was done by little children so quick that it was impossible to discover completely how it was done - and our next and last sight was proceeded to without my ready conception of the preceding one - this next was how the heads were made - which was thus - a long strip of wire, the thickness of the pin, was fastened to a fixture, - and then some thinner wire was put on it - a little girl, then, held that wire round which some of a thinner texture was put, under her arm, - and by means of a sort of spinning machine wound it round the thicker, quite close, like silk when wound round a roller - the thick wire was, then, pulled out, and the same little girl, not above twelve years old, cut it off by partitions of two, to the size of the heads and the Pin was thus completed ; - the whole process of which

*afforded a most interesting sight. - We then went to see Thom...
. . .where we saw the Warwick vase and finished our day by dining at Mr Boulton's. ---*

On Wednesday - the 31st Soon after we had breakfasted, Mr Wheeler and his son called upon us, to offer their services in taking us to the different manufactories, which we readily accepted, and accordingly set out accompanied by young Mr Wheeler only to see these different manufactories. And, when we had enquired at the Post office about some letters, we proceeded directly to the Nail manufactory, which is a most curious and interesting process, but one that I could not sufficiently comprehend to give a description of, and shall accordingly pass on to another, which I am more familiar with. From the Nail manufactory we had intended to proceed & see the Glass one, but it being the dinner time for the workmen, we only settled with the man, that we should see it at a later hour: and in the mean time took some refreshment at old Mr Wheeler's after which we visit his Gun manufactory, which afforded more interest to myself than any of the rest had done : and I accordingly made myself pretty perfect in it; - so much so that I shall attempt to explain how a Gun is made. - The first process is, that a great number of horse - shoe nails are collected together - these, then, are enclosed in an inferior iron - hoop in the form of a horse - shoe - after which this hoop is put into a furnace, where it becomes as hot as possible - and by being made so hot, it is possible - by degrees - and putting it into the fire fifty or sixty times - to form it into a long iron bar, which is effected by hammering it, when it is in it's highest state of heat - when, then, this iron bar is completed - the next process, is, to twist it, - which is done by making this small bar red hot - and then winding it upon another round bar, as you would draw up a barge - mast, which will complete the twisting.

- *What, then, follows, is, that this twisting should be so united, the one twist to the other, that it would be impossible to make any division whatever - which is effected, by putting an iron pole, the size of the muzzle of a common gun, through the middle of the twist, - and then thrusting the whole into the furnace, and as you bring it out, perpetually hammering it, while the rod is still in, and afterwards, as you draw it out, forcing the different twists, which are then red hot, together, which is obtained by perpetual hammering - After, then, this has been done sixty or seventy times, the barrel, for it then becomes one, is ready to be ground, which is done as you would grind a knife, after which it has to be bored - which is effected in the following way. - The barrel is fixed at the one end on a long form or table by means of a vice - and a long iron - pole sharp at two square sides with a piece of wood put on the top of it to force the sharp side to the barrel is played upon by means of another machine, like a gim blet, till it has gone thro' the whole barrel, which makes it completely round and smooth inside. - Thus far did we see a Gun completed. -*

We next proceeded to visit the Glass manufactory, which afforded very great amusement to us, - yet, I am sorry to say such an amusement as it is impossible, owing to the very many different experiments and exhibitions presented, for me to describe, but I will endeavour to make up for this, by giving as good an account as I am able of our next manufactory, which was the "Whip".-The first process of making which, is, a square long piece of Whalebone is prepared - pieces of Cane, round on one side and flat on the other, are then fastened, by means of pitch, to each side of this whalebone - the flat side being next the whalebone - and the round outside - so that it, then, appears, quite round - but it is not fast - and in order to make it so, a pitched cord is put on at the end of the whalebone, (surrounded by the cane) - and so worked round it, as to press the cane as close as possible to the Whalebone - so as to make it almost inseparable - but - at the same time - owing to the different parts it is formed of-elastic it is, then, forwarded to a machine, where it is made into the form in which you buy it, that is - covered over with very fine string - Thus ended our sights at Birmingham, for it was then, time for us to go to dinner, which we had at Mr Wheeler's, where we were most hospitably entertained - and after spending a very pleasant evening there, we went to our Hotel and packed up for our journey to "Chester" the next morning.-----------

On Thursday - the first of August - We set out from Birmingham on our journey to "Chester" - it was about six o'clock when we started and the first three or four miles out of Birmingham was very uninteresting - until we got to Wednesbury, where our attention was diverted -not by the fine country - for it was anything but that - but the immense number of coal pits and their works - it is unnecessary to add that it is here, where the Stafford - Shire coal is procured - but the smoke proceeding from these mines is so thick and black that it completely darkens the Atmosphere, and emits a considerable share of it's odour - The machines, too, are very curious, and worked by steam - and you will frequently see, in the midst of the smoke, flames of fire blazing out at the Chimneys: - These coalmines and works cover the country from "Wednesbury" to Wolverhampton, where we breakfasted - As you enter this place you see before you, and pass by on your left hand the remains of an old Castle, formerly called Wolverhampton Castle, but now formed into a Japan manufactory: - the town itself is large and narrow, and not interesting, but- for this omission here you are amply repaid, when you approach the village of "King's Tettenhall", where the Church and village, and houses on a

Coalbrookdale

height, quite opposite to you, which you afterwards pass on your right hand, afford a most picturesque and interesting view, surrounded as the whole is by fine and lofty timber. - After, then, you have ascended a very steep and long hill, you come into some park - scenery, and travel, completely surrounded by trees, having a view, on your left, of a fine country seat. - You, soon after this, have a very extensive scene exhibited to you, - when you see, on your right, the Raikin , which you will, afterwards, pass close under, on your left, - now sixteen miles distant - then - on the left - a very open scene of fine rich country - and part of Worcestershire (as the Coachman stated) - the whole being a most beautiful sight. - You, likewise, pass Bonningale, which is so small, that you would scarcely observe it - after which you approach to "Shiffnall", - and as you enter it, you are presented with a fine view of a church, on the high ground,- a handsome house and grounds above it - overlooking it - as well as some gentleman's seats on the right hand - all which are very striking - and after you have passed through the town, you have a fuller view of the Church, and the house that before overlooked you. - As, then, you proceed you have a very distant and scarcely perceptable view of Tongue-Castle, the property of George Durant Esqu, who, upon being separated from his wife, erected a monument, which you, likewise, have a sight of. - Some distance further from this place you come to Oaken Gates and Ketter where there is a great iron - foundry - if too, you look back on your left, you see where Colebrook dale is situated, being at this place no great distance from it: - You likewise have, on your left, Raekin close to you, - the ground under it being covered with coal mines. = We, then, changed horses at Hay - Gate, a little distance from which you are presented with a most magnificent scene - and, for the first time, have a very distant view of the Welsh Mountains - and a sight of Shrewsbury, and even Lord Hill's column, eight miles distant from you - The whole scene affording a magnificent - extensive - and luxuriant view. - You likewise have Wellington on your right hand: - the church of which place, as you go on, and look back, is a very pretty object rising out of some trees. - After having, for some distance, been indulged with the extensive view I have above mentioned, we came into level ground andmore enclosed country, - and had a view of Attingham house, Lord Berwick's which is a very noble and handsome building, resembling very much, in shape and situation the Earl of Portsmouth's, near Andover, Hants.

The next place, that attracted our notice was Atcham, which is very delightfully situated on the banks of the Severn; which we here cross, for the first time, having, from the bridge, a view of the church, which is very pretty, and close upon the banks of the river. - From this place, you ride along the banks of the river for a considerable distance, till you come to where it makes a great wind, where you have a very fine reach of the

Shrewsbury, 1830

stream, with the trees close upon it's edge; - when you lose sight of it till you come to "Shrewsbury". The whole way to which, is very interesting, being in distance about a mile and a half. The entrance into Shrewsbury is very fine - You pass close to Lord Hills pillar, which is a very handsome structure - and as you go into the town, - you pass over a fine bridge across the Severn, and on your right, as you are crossing, you have a fine view of the castle and the jail - which are situated on a lofty hill - you likewise have a fine reach of the river. - Directly, then, that you have passed the bridge, you ascend the town by a very steep - hill, - at the top of which was our Inn - where we dined, having to remain at Shrewsbury for an hour, owing to the change of Coaches. - As, then, this was the case we strolled about the town to see as much as we could in so short a time. - We, accordingly, went up the principal street, as I conceive, in which our inn was .. and on the left, as you go up, is the market - and town hall - the former being a very old building - The whole square space, was at this time, very much crowded, *owing to the circumstance of the assizes, which were then going on. - We then saw one or two of the Churches, after which it was time for us to go to our coach, upon which we had to remain a long time in the yard - owing to a disputation about places - at the same time that we encountered a great deal of impudence from the proprietor; - however, we, at last, proceeded on our journey - and passed nearer the Castle, than we yet had. - On the right as you go out of "Shrewsbury", the church of Patterfield is a very pretty sight - and a very little further on, on the same side of the road, is the very little cottage church of Eberton, and on the left, in the distance is Brixwell hill, and still far ther, the hills of Montgomery Shire, beyond which are the Denbigh, affording a very fine extensive view - (you have, likewise on the road, a great many little cottages) As, then, you proceed you leave Pimmel hill close to your left, but before you leave it, and are still opposite to it - you have a fine hilly - as well as level - country on your right - a windmill affording a picturesque object. - You have likewise behind you a sight of Raikin. - and when you proceed a little further - you again have a view of the Welsh mountains in the distance, and a fine prospect on the left - You, then, go along a fir plantation, from which, on your left, you have an extensive view with the hill of Pemmel, and when you come to the end of the plantation, you are presented witha more magnificent and nearer view of the Montgomery and Denbigh hills, with a most extensive foreground all about you - and the Cheshire hills on your right - the whole, together, exhibiting a most beautiful and luxuriant scene. = All this is between Shrewsbury and Burton. - from which place the scenery is still, I remember, very striking but I do not recollect it enough to describe it, excepting towards the end of the stage where you see a beautiful piece of Water, with an extensive back view - but, upon ascending the hill the scene is particularly striking - as you have a most impressive view of a Windmill and Ellesmere church rising up out of the midst of a hill - with another very woody hill, close in front of you - and a little further on just before you enter Ellesmere you have a fine piece of water, - after passing which you find yourself in the small - but neat town of Ellesmere , where we changed horses, and proceeded on our journey for "Wrexham" . And here I have to regret that I cannot fully describe the magnificent scenery we passed through. - but I will endeavour to recollect as much as I can. - Till you come to Oberton the whole country is very beautiful and delightful just before you enter this village - the scenery, I conceive, is almost beyond description, even where you upon the spot to give it. - You ascend a hill from whence you look down upon a most extensive and richly cultivated valley - the timber and foliage are most most rich and luxuriant - houses scattered about, seem as if they built on purpose to be seen from this elevated spot. Some you will see situated on the side of a hill, that is on the side of - and runs down into the valley - surrounded completely excepting their roofs, with trees and the richest foliage - others you will see - down in the bottom of the valley - not destitute of wood - but showing more of themselves - and surrounded by corn and hay-fields, filled with reapers and gleaners - others again are encompassed by meadow -ground, where, in the place of reapers, you see sheep and oxen. - but the beauty of the valley does not end here - for in the midst of all the luxuriant ground, that I have very poorly described, you enjoy the sight of the river Dee winding most beautifully - and, in most places, surrounded by very rich green meadows - which are close to the stream. = One would think, that such a scene could not have an additional beautiful feature, - or that there could be any improvement - but, perhaps, you will allow that there is an additional feature and improvement, when you hear, that you have, in the distance, a view of the Welsh mountains, which make a very good boundary to the valley - and here they appear to greater effect, than we had yet seen them - for independent of being situated as they have been described, the sun was shining most brilliantly on their grey sides. - Such was the country that we saw upon our entry into "Wales". - And it is not only from one particular spot that we saw all this luxuriant country - but we took a circuit - on this high terrace - so that we had a view, at a distance, of what we were a moment back upon - besides a different sight of the valley below us. - I must not omit to state that the property of Sir Watkin Wynn lies in this valley. = Upon our leaving all this most beautiful scenery, we come immediately into the village of Overton, where, I am happy to say we stopped for a short time to water our horses - for here too, it was most beautiful altho' in a different way. - We had just crossed the river Dee, and were stopping almost upon the bridge, from whence we looked down the stream, which was most beautiful, - and had a hill above us, filled with cottages and little gardens. - The scenery of which I cannot describe, but*

St Giles's Church, Wrexham

only say that it was most interesting and attractive.

From hence we journeyed on to "Wrexham", the whole road to which was most interesting, and very pretty altho' very much inferior to what we had passed. When we arrived here we were welcomed by the sight of rather a large town - not very interesting excepting for it's church, which is a most beautiful one - and situated on a high hill, overlooking the town. - We, then, proceeded on our journey, till, after passing thro' a great deal of Denbigh Shire and some very fine scenery we arrived at "Chester" about 8 oclock, passing by in our way Eaton the seat of Lord Grosvenor, which appears to be a most magnificent mansion. - As you look through the gates to the house, it appears as if it was not above half a mile distant from you, when in reality it is two miles and a half up to the house from the Gates. Directly we arrived at Chester we made our preparations for the night, having determined not to start till five o clock the next afternoon, thus allowing ourselves time to see this curious old place. Thus ended our day's journey from Birmingham to Chester.

And I must add, that I was never so much delighted with any, as with this. - The country we had passed was most beautiful and luxuriant - and where it was not so, it was curious, such, for instance, as among the coal mines, - it was curious and interesting. At the former part of the day we found it very cold - but afterwards, it altered and became very warm - and beautiful - and I found nothing to complain of - but the want of time to survey the very beautiful country that presented itself to our view: and which equalled any thing that I ever saw.

Friday. August. 2nd = Before breakfast we took a walk round the walls of Chester, - but as I shall describe these a little further on I shall proceed to relate what we did immediately after breakfast. - In our passage round the walls

Wrexham

we had purchased a "Stranger's guide in Chester", with which we started to see the town. - I believe that there was not one street that escaped our notice. - We set off from our Inn, which was called the Hotel, in Eastgate Street, and went regularly round the town; for which trouble we felt ourselves amply repaid. - It is one of the oldest towns, I believe, in the kingdom, and has retained it's old-fashioned buildings up to the present day. - These curious houses afford much interest to the traveller. - not only on account of the long time that they have existed, but on account of the manner in which they are built - and the material that forms them. - The greater part of them consisting of wood, which appears, where there is any other material, in different divisions. - But what is most to be observed in Chester, is, what are called "Rows". Here, there are not, as in most other towns, paths, by the sides of the streets, but all is carriage road, so that in a description, you might fancy, that there was no accomodation for foot passengers: - this, however, is not the case - for it is in these Rows, that I have mentioned, that foot passengers find their place for walking - unmolested by any thing but human beings unless a dog or cat happen sometimes

The Rows, Chester

to produce themselves. This description of these Rows, however, being attended with greater difficulty and requiring a longer duration of time -, than I am able to afford = I shall copy it out of my little guide book, which, I can affirm, is a very accurate one. = These Rows, "says my Chester Guide", appear somewhat, as if the front room of the first floor, in every house, was taken out, and the upper part of the premises, supported on pillars; while the lower tier of rooms are occupied as shops. The space thus left, becomes a kind of gallery on each side of the street, fenced in front with an irregular balustrading or railing; and the back is converted into a row of shops, which are considered the principal in the town, and very much frequented, from the great convenience of passing from street to street, effectually secured from the unpleasantness of rain or excessive heat. These Rows, altho' formed on a general plan, are far from being uniform, their height being only in proportion to each respective house tho' the flooring is tolerably level; so that in some places a tall man is obliged to stoop a little, while, in others, there may be one, two or three feet above him. This want of regularity, however, corresponds so well with general appearances, that it renders it rather pleasing than otherwise. For public accommodation, there are stone or wood steps, at every forty or fifty yards to go down into the street, so that no one need be exposed longer than while crossing. Such is my Guide's description of the Rows, which are so interesting and curious. In the course of our traversing we came to the Cathedral, which, altho' very unlike any other I had ever seen, yet is a very fine and handsome one in my opinion, altho' I have heard it abused. It is built of the Redstone, that is so plentiful in that part of the country which, I think, is by no means displeasing to the sight, altho' I do not mean to compare it to the fine stone, which forms the greater part of our Cathedrals. In the first place it is a stone of a sandy substance, and therefore sooner perishable, owing to which you see many fresh scratches in the walls of the building then its very colour takes something away from the idea of a Cathedral. But I do not dislike singularity a specimen of which, I think, this Cathedral is, and well worthy the notice of any traveller. The next thing we saw was the Castle, which is a very fine building, part being old, part new the one equal with the Christian era the other of very late date: Thus ended our examination of Chester having

Chester Cathedral

started from Eastgate, and walked till we came round to it again when my father went into the hotel to write a letter and I put my ink paper and pens into my pocket and started, a second time, for the walls, having been, in the morning so delighted with the view, that I was determined to describe it, as I was sitting on the walls. which is contained in the following words. = From the wall, just opposite the new part of the Castle, you look down upon the Race course, called Rhoodee, which is in the form of an Amphitheatre and well adapted, from its situation as to the walls, for the spectator's seeing the races. On the opposite side of the course, is an acclivity covered with short trees, between which and the course, the Dee, a sight of which you have on your left, flows and beyond that you have a most beautiful scene over the country, with the Welsh mountains in the distance, which you see in a range right and left on the highest of which you see Foxe's monument. The whole before you appears as if it was painted grey or rather sky colour the sun, at the time that I was viewing the scenery, shining full upon it. What you see in Wales, is, Flint, Denbigh and Montgomery-shire. The view from this part of the Walls appeared to me most beautiful, but, as I proceeded to my right, I think, the scenery, which is nearly the same is finer from that part of the wall, where the Water tower is in as much as, you have a more extensive foreground and the Welsh mountains appear as if they were nearer the river likewise, where you see some ships, winds immediately under you but now, which is not of much consequence with regard to the scenery you lose sight of Rhoodee and it wants the improvement of the houses, immediately opposite, being removed, as they now disfigure it. As, however, you advance towards the Northgate you have a very far superior and more extensive view from an eminence called Morgan's mount, You see more of the Dee as well as of the forground, which is most beautiful appearing to rise more gradually, till it reaches the Welsh mountains themselves. From this point, it is indeed most impressive and attractive and ought always to be viewed the last, as it is by far the finest and impossible to be compared with the other views. The fine range of Welsh mountains give the distant outline, in which may be perceived the Jubilee column, (Foxe's monument) on MoelTanema; the middle and foreground is occupied by Hawarden church and Castle and the venerable ruins of Flint Castle with the Dee. The wood of all you look down upon is very rich and plentiful, altho', in this respect, not equal to what you look down upon from Richmond Hill. No one, that is an admirer of fine open scenery, can help admiring this altho' he may, at the same time feel, that he has seen finer. As, then, you proceed in your walk round the walls, you pass by Phoenix tower, from whence you look over Cheshire on your left and have a fine view of the Cathedral close to you on your right after passing which you come to Eastgate, when it was time for dinner.

After dinner, we proceeded, about 5 o clock, in a coach to Eastham ferry, where we joined a steamboat, which took us to Liverpool, where we slept that night forgoing any examination of this town, as we should have to visit it on our return from the Lakes. When we arrived, the first thing we did was to enquire about our means of reaching Keswick the next day. There was no Steam boat, that stopt at Whitehaven. So that our water expedition was put an end to we then applied for places in a Coach when we found there was no room I then, proposed, that we should go to Manchester where we might be more lucky, which after some deliberation, was agreed to, and we took inside places in a two horsed auxiliary mail, which started at five o clock the next morning for Manchester. We then went to

Eastham Ferry

our inn, which was the King's Arms, had some tea and went to bed. The weather during the whole of this day, had been most favourable for us.==========

Saturday August 3rd = Started at 5 o'clock this morning, for Manchester, where we arrived, after having passed over "thirty six" miles of very uninteresting country, at "nine" o'clock and breakfasted at the Bridgewater Arms, after which, we went to take our places in a coach to Lancaster, which was to start from the Star Inn at "one" --- In the mean, we strolled about to see what we could of the town: and I called upon my friend "John Hull" in Mosely street, who very kindly acted towards as a guide; and would have shown us one of the cotton manufactories, but the Man to whom the manufactory belonged, being out, he was prevented; -finding then, that we could not manage this we went to see the place where the riots happened, which is in Peter's fields but which has lately changed its name, owing to the famous battle there, into "Peterloo", in imitation of Waterloo. We then, resumed our walk thro' the streets without finding much to attract our notice. We, likewise visited the exchange, which is in the form of an Amphitheatre, by which

The Bridgewater Arms, Manchester

time, it became necessary for us to join our coach, which we did, and having taken leave of my friend we proceeded on our journey to Lancaster.

As we went out of Manchester we passed by the Crescent which is composed of very comfortable houses beautifully situated on high ground overlooking the river Irwell and the town. Three or four miles further, or perhaps less you have a very extensive view with the Lancashire hills at a little distance, and you look down upon a fine valley in which is the village of Ringley with a very picturesque bridge soon after which you come to Bolton from which place, all the way to "Blackburn" the country is anything but pretty. It is very hilly bad roads and dreary and desolate it was not, however, uninteresting, because it was such a complete contrast to what we had been and led one to contemplate on the past scenery from the peculiarity and barrenness of the present. After passing through two or three stages of this country we arrived at "Blackburn", where we stayed some time, altho' we only changed horses. I took a very great deal of pleasure in being in this place as I often had talked about it- and heard a great deal of it not owing to any thing peculiar in the town itself but on account of its' being the home of one of my most intimate and kindest friends. Often have I heard him speak of Old-Blackburn when, perhaps, we were in the midst of a fine speech in "Thucydides" -and as often have I wished to visit it. The person I allude to is H.S. Cardwell. who is a real good fellow and a firm friend and it is with pleasure I state, that I often think of him, when I am reading those books, with which I must be familiar before I take my degree. in as much as I have, on a former occasion, read the greater part of them with him. This, then, was the circumstance, which made me so glad to enter "Blackburn". I asked at Brennand's one of the shops, where my friend lived, who told me that it was in King street but, as I thought, we should only stay two or three minutes longer, I did not attempt to call upon him which, had I known beforehand, how long we were to stay, I could easily have done. In our way out we passed thro' King street, but I could not find out the House. I observed to myself that the country before you come to, and about Blackburn was very ugly but I am happy to say, for the credit of my friend a little way on you pass a very pretty spot. You come to a Bridge with a waterfall and a rock with some rich trees and fine foliage overhanging it and a little further on you have a very picturesque object on your right with a steep hill in front of you ascending which, you have a pretty sight on your left as you cross a bridge you see a hill mostly covered with wood and part quite bare, hanging over the stream when, then, you have mounted the hill you must look back and you have a very pretty view of Mr Fielding's. Pursuing your journey you have a view of Hoghton hall on your right, where Charles the first

Hoghton Hall

concealed himself when so persecuted as he was by Cromwell. After this, as you descend a hill, which is Hoghton Lane about 4 miles from Blackburn you have a most beautiful and extensive view both of level country and very fine hills, with Hoghton tower on your right and on your left a view of the sea with a sight of Preston about six miles off. After this the country on to Preston is less attractive yet still pretty, especially as you approach within a mile and a half of this place. As you enter Preston you see a fine house of Lord Derby's on your right and as you proceed into the town you have the church on your left. Here we dined and stayed about one hour, having to wait for a Liverpool coach to come up upon which we were to proceed to Lancaster. In the mean time we went back to the point where we entered Preston to see the view, which was behind us, as we came in, but which was very pretty and greatly improved upon the second sight of it by the rays of the setting sun shining upon the scenery. After we had been absent a short time we returned and put ourselves on our new Coach, upon which we had

scarcely room to sit it was so full, owing to the two coaches meeting. We however proceeded, most uncomfortably through Garstang to Lancaster, where we arrived about "eleven" o clock at night. Not being able to discover what sort of Country it was we passed through from Preston. Directly we arrived we had some porter and went to bed, determining to remain, the former part of next day, at Lancaster.
===========

Sunday August 4th = After breakfast we went to Church, where we obtained a very comfortable large seat to ourselves, and heard the service, admirably performed in every department and when it was ended we took a survey of the inside of the church, which is very fine, having a very handsome altar piece, something similar to the one in Eton Chapel it has, likewise, a very handsome and fine toned organ, behind which is some sculpture: indeed the whole church, inside and out, is a very magnificent building. Directly after church we strolled about the yard, and admired the view. We then mounted the steps leading up to the castle, and walked along till we came round to the large gates when we knocked at the door to enquire whether we could see the castle, and being answered in the affirmative we went round and saw the various stations for the different prisoners than which nothing can be more healthy and clean we afterwards proceeded to John of Gaunt's tower, from which we had a most beautiful prospect for, on the left, as you get up, you have a view of Sunderland point, and the mouth of the Loyne, with the sea at the boundary, the breeze of which comes freshly upon you then as you, by degrees, to your right, you look over the Loyne on to the Lancaster Sands, the other side of which are the Cumberland and Westmorland mountains, at the extreme point of which line of land is Peel castle, situated on an island. As you advance and have turned the corner you

Lancaster Castle and Church

look down upon the church and have a view of the new bridge and the Aqueduct, with the Westmorland mountains in the distance, and, likewise, Engleborough hill on the borders of Yorkshire, the water, immediately underneath you, adding to the beauty of the scene without any necessity of what you have, namely, the looking down upon the felons and other prisoners in the castle. The next turning brings you to a view of Cloptr Pike Lancaster town, which looks exceedingly well and the debtors close under you with the governour's house: turning again, you have a view of the sea, and the shipping on the Loyne; and, when you ascend John of Gaunt's chair, you have the entire view North East South and West at once the whole presenting a most beautiful Panoramic scene. After this we went to see the Court rooms, which are very handsome, especially the Civil one: and, then, quitting the Castle, we examined the town, which is, in my opinion, the nicest we had passed through: the houses are mostly, indeed I may say all, built of the same stone as the Castle and nothing can be cleaner or more comfortable size than the streets :and there is a square with some very excellent houses: ===== All this we observed in our way to the bridge, which is very handsome and built like Waterloo, quite straight across the river equal arched: from thence there is a fine view of the church and Castle: we, then, after taking a turn down a very pretty lounging walk, visited the quay, upon which are the Warehouses (very good ones) having then walked some way, feeling a fine breeze, we returned and partook of a cold dinner, when we had some most excellently dressed potatoes, for which Lancashire is famous, and some very good rich cream with our tart. I must add, before I quit Lancaster, that it has a fine townhall in the marketplace, where our Inn, the Royal Oak was. Having, thus, given, as well as I can, a true account of the country about, and town of, Lancaster, I must not omit, to mention another thing, which it, in common with Lancashire, in general, has to boast of and that is the beauty of it's females. I had frequently heard of the Lancashire witches, famed for their beauty but now I saw them, and, I can, with truth, alledge, that I never met with so many pretty girls modest girls as I did here and the country about. It is not ladies, that I am speaking of, for, I scarcely saw any, but cottagers farmer's daughters and servants. Their dress altho' it was Sunday, was quiet and becoming no flowers in their bonnets no flounces on their gowns, which you sometimes see among the maid servants in the South: but their dress was neat and simple and their demeanor becoming their station: When I passed them, they hung down their heads and when I attempted to look behind at them, for which I sometimes overtook them, they turned away from me, which forced me to admire them. And I fancied I saw a real innocent pretty country girl. In many places beauty and simplicity live beneath a cottage roof but here particularly. As we passed from Lancaster to Kendal I saw some of the prettiest girls, I had ever seen, standing at their different cottage doors, not daring, as it were, to look up to the coach and frequently running in doors and flying from the windows. Thus it is, that Modesty and Humility will gain admirers where Beauty and Pride thwart and destroy their own selves: Give me the cottage, where Simplicity and Humility reside, rather than the palace of Pride and extreme beauty. Thus much of Lancaster .===

After we had dined we proceeded about four o clock, on our way to Kendal, the whole of which road is very interesting, more especially after you leave Milthorpe; however, a very little way out of Lancaster, you have, on your left, a very extensive view of the sea, with the sands, and the Westmorland mountains especially those, which, afterwards, a little further on, before you enter Bolton, appear still finer: they prepare you a little for what you afterwards have to encounter: Beyond this, however, the country as far as Milthorpe is not particularly attractive.

Milnthorpe

Kendal

but when you quit this place, it is most beautiful and rich the whole way to Kendal : soon after you get out of Milthorpe you come to a village called Eversham, which is particularly pretty: You have, a little way out of it, on your left hand, the house of Coln Howard, and a little beyond this you come upon a bridge, which is very picturesque on the right side where you see a stream winding down through rich trees, with a small hill above, and on the other side, the same water is observed flowing in a troubled manner over stones, with a view of the Westmorland mountains. In fact, the whole way from Milthorpe to Kendal is most beautiful: the road itself, when you loose the mountains, is most plentifully surrounded with trees and green luxuriant meadows being every now and then favoured with a sight of the lost mountains. At no great distance from Kendal and near the road side, you pass Sizergh, the property of Mr Strickland, a very fine old house situated in a parkland surrounded by great deal of timber:- = There is, in this house, a room, in which, it is said, Queen Mary, once slept, which is

Sizergh Hall

still kept, bed and all, in the state that it then was, but now a useless room. We, then, arrived, after passing through very pretty country, at Kendal, which is situated in a valley, surrounded by hills:- As you enter it, there is a bridge a cross the river Kent, which you pass by on your right, and, then, proceed down a long clean street till you come to the King's Arms, where we slept.==========

The next morning, Monday 5th, we got up very early, and went in search of Scout Scar, a rock, from whence, it is said, is a very fine view but, having no prospect of finding it and being tied down to the Coach time which was soon we returned and had our breakfast, by which time, the coach was ready, on which we proceeded to "Ambleside"; in the road to which, we for first time, come in among the Westmorland mountains, which by degrees, begin to surround you, till you come to the Lake of Windere-Mere, which is most beautiful. On first approaching it

Windermere

you see very little of its' expansive water but the high mountains and gentler hills about it the small white houses close upon its' bank and the smoothness of its' water are most exquisitely beautiful. As, then, you proceed, you have, in front of you, a most magnificent view of Mountains, intermingled with each other one as it were giving rise to another and each ascending with different hues the sun shining brilliantly on one a black cloud immediately overhanging another: here, crowded with trees and green plats there, nothing but rock and barrenness. = From this magnificent sight, you are again, after having passed through a great deal of wood, introduced to Windermere, where you see the greater part of its' expanse but only the greater part for, never, owing to its' winding and length, can it be seen all at once. = Here you find yourself at Ambleside, which appears to be a place very much frequented by travellers, who are in their way to and from the Lakes: it is very pleasantly situated, a very little way from Windermere lake and has a very fine large Inn is

Rydal Quarries

fourteen miles from Kendal and sixteen from "Keswick". = Having changed horses and coachmen, we proceeded to Keswick, passing through, I should conceive, the finest sixteen miles of Country in England. Going out of Ambleside you descend a very awkward and steep hill, when you get on to somewhat level-ground, and pass over a very pretty road you then cross a small stream and come upon Rydal lake, which is but a small yet pretty lake it has two islands close together and is surrounded with woody hills = excepting on your right, where there are slate quarries passing by which, you have to ascend a steep and rough hill, which brings you to Grasmere-lake. Before, however, you indulge yourself, with a sight of this you must look back upon Rydal, which looks very well from the hill. The slate quarries, on yr left, by no means disfigure the scenery = Now you may gratify yourself with receiving Grass-Mere, which is considerably larger than Rydal, and a finer lake altogether. There is one solitary green island in it upon which a

Thirlmere

shed is built, they sometimes put sheep upon it, which must be an improvement but, as there were none upon it when we passed, I cannot be a judge, excepting from imagination this lake, like all the rest is surrounded by mountains. When, then, you leave Grasmere, you are introduced to a most thorough barren and mountainous country, No trees present themselves to your view nothing but rocky mountains and hills with scarce any grass upon them. You would suppose that no living thing was near you, did you not every now and then see the shepherd attending upon his sheep.- You hear the mountain torrents rushing down all about you you observe large masses of Rock, which have rolled, some time or other from the tops of the surrounding mountains in one place you may, unexpectedly be treated with the sight of a poor solitary lifeless tree in another with the view of a little corn-field, which appears as if it would never have an ear to boast of. Such is the barrenness you meet with upon quitting Gras-mere. But, yet, this barrenness is far *from being disinteresting it is such a contrast to what you have been through that it works upon your feelings it makes you wonder, how it is possible, that you could so instantaneously, almost, be removed from the most luxuriant and woody scenery to the most desolate and rocky country:-that, here, you should see a wide expanse of water as smooth as glass and without a bubble there a small stream rushing down and carrying every thing before it, with incessant noise.- Having passed over a great deal of this desolate tract up and down steep hills, you come to the division of the counties of "Cumberland" and "Westmorland", which is a long stone wall down the hills on each side of you. The view of the Cumberland Mountains is very magnificent and very different from those we had passed. After having proceeded a little way into Cumberland, you come close under "Helvellin", on your right. It is a fine lofty and rocky mountain and very grand it is 3055 feet above the level of the sea. Soon after this you come to the Lake of Thurlmere or Leeswater, which is very magnificent and very different to the ones we had already seen It is very long and almost in a straight line, from end to end. You have it close on the left of you for about "two miles the road being alongside of it. It appears much longer than it really is owing to its' being so narrow it has one very little bush of an island and about the middle of it there is a bridge across it, where it is very narrow. The whole length, I believe, is "four" miles. The mountains come down more precipately into this lake, than they did into the others, we had passed this of course is on your left hand, and on the other side of the lake on the right you have Helvellin overhanging you. = As, then, you leave the lake, and proceed through the mountains you have a fine sight of "Saddleback" in front of you at some distance from it. You then take a turn to your left have another glimpse of Thurlemere behind you, and are, again, enclosed*

Keswick: Greta Hall and Keswick bridge.

within the mountains. Saddleback being immediately before you. You, then, go on a little further, and have a magnificent sight still of Saddleback, but on your right and "Skiddaw" in front of you. Two fine fellows they are Soon after this you have a view first, of Bassenthwaite lake before you, and, then, of Derwent water, on your left, at the same time that you look down into and upon the vale and town of "Keswick" over which you see Skiddaw hanging most gloriously a few moments more brings you into the town of Keswick, where we found "Mr Southey" at the Inn all ready to receive us. He and my father proceeded immediately to his house, which is situated at the other end of the town I waited to accompany the baggage; which did not long delay me; and I found myself in Mr Southey's house about "quarter past three". when I was introduced to his wife and his eldest daughter "Edith". After then sitting with them for a short time, we went and prepared ourselves for dinner which was to be at "four", the familie's

Greta Hall

regular dinner hour. Having made myself comfortable I returned to the study where I was introduced to Mrs Coleridge and her daughter "Sara", I was likewise introduced to Dr Bell, who had come in the same coach with my father and myself from Rydal, and had taken lodgings at Keswick. Our dinner and evening went off very delightfully and after supper, which was always at half-past nine, I was very glad to adjourn to bed. = Thus ended the last day of our journey: and it was with no small degree of pleasure that I hailed my home of three weeks. There is always a pleasure and satisfaction in arriving at a resting place after roaming about and altho' my travelling had not caused the fatigue which some experience or taken up as much time as a voyage to Rio Janeiro would still I was very glad to find myself at that spot, where all further travelling was to cease for a time, and have an opportunity of re= =calling what has past.

not long delay me; – and I found myself
in Mr Southey's house about a quarter past
three; – when I was introduced to his wife
and his oldest daughter "Edith". After then
sitting with them for a short time, we
went and prepared ourselves for dinner
which was to be at "four". The family's
regular dinner hour. – Having made my-
-self comfortable, I returned to the study where
I was introduced to Mrs Coleridge and her
daughter "Sara". I was likewise introduced
to Dr Bell, who had come in the same
coach with my father and myself from
Rydal, and had taken lodgings at Kes-
-ick. – Our dinner and evening went off
very delightfully – and after supper, which
was always at half-past nine, I was very
glad to adjourn to Bed. – Thus ended
the last day of our journey: – and it was with
no small degree of pleasure that I hailed my
tome of these-works. – There is always
a pleasure and satisfaction in arriving at a
resting-place after roaming about – and al-
-tho' my travelling had not caused the fa-
-tigue, which some experience – or taken
up as much time as a voyage to Rio
Janeiro would – still I was very glad
to find myself at that spot, where all
further travelling was to cease for a

CATALOGUE

OF

A VALUABLE ASSEMBLAGE

OF

BOOKS,

INCLUDING

THE LIBRARY OF THE LATE JOHN MAY, Esq.

OF BLACKHEATH,

COMPRISING

Some Valuable Historical & General Works in English Literature,

RARE BOOKS AND CHRONICLES,

VOYAGES AND TRAVELS,

ANTIQUARIAN PUBLICATIONS,

REPRINTS OF CURIOUS AND RARE FRENCH PIECES,

BY TECHENER,

FINE BOOKS OF PRINTS AND COSTUMES,

CURIOUS AND RARE WORKS ON QUAKERISM,

A most Valuable and Extensively Illustrated Copy

OF THE

BEAUTIES OF ENGLAND, WALES AND SCOTLAND,

In 76 Vols. on large paper, bound in red morocco extra,

A FEW INTERESTING MANUSCRIPTS,

WORKS RELATING TO AMERICA,

An Extensive Collection of Wood Engravings,

EARLY EDITIONS OF THE CLASSICS,

&c. &c.

WHICH WILL BE SOLD BY AUCTION,

BY MESSRS.

S. LEIGH SOTHEBY & JOHN WILKINSON,

AUCTIONEERS OF LITERARY PROPERTY AND WORKS ILLUSTRATIVE OF THE FINE ARTS,

AT THEIR HOUSE, 3, WELLINGTON STREET, STRAND,

On MONDAY, 10th of NOVEMBER, 1856, and Four following Days,

AT ONE O'CLOCK PRECISELY.

May be Viewed on Friday and Saturday previous, and Catalogues had.

The Auction catalogue for John May's Library.

References

ABBREVIATIONS
H.R.O.   Hampshire Record Office
Rev C.C. Southey. The Life and Correspondence of Robert Southey - Rev C. C. Southey - 1851.
Ramos: The Letters of Robert Southey to John May 1797 to 1838. Edited with an Introduction by CHARLES RAMOS Jenkins Publishing Company, The Pemberton Press, Austin, 1976
Lord Coleridge - 1905 The Story of a Devonshire House - Lord Coleridge - 1905.
Warter: Selections from the Letters of Robert Southey - Warter - 1856
Victoria STC: Samuel Taylor Coleridge Collection, Victoria University Library (Toronto).

Ref. No   Reference
1 H.R.O. - 2M69.
2 The Common Place Book of John May. (Private collection.)
3 The Common Place Book of John May.
4 The Common Place Book of John May.
5 H.R.O. - 2M69.
6 The British Factory in Lisbon. A R Walford. 1940, 60.
7 Extract from Joseph May's Pocket Book. (Private collection.)
8 The Common Place Book of John May.
9 The Common Place Book of John May.
10 The British Factory in Lisbon. A R Walford. 1940, 59.
11 The Common Place Book of John May.
12 The Common Place Book of John May.
13 The British Factory in Lisbon. A R Walford. 1940, 72.
14 H.R.O. - 2M69.
15 The British Factory in Lisbon. A R Walford.1940, 121.
16 Gentleman's Magazine,201(Jul-Dec,1856)124 Col 2.
17 Robert Southey a Life - Mark Storey - 1997, 1.
18 Victoria STC, 815, (17.2), (15-12-1793).
19 Victoria STC, 815, (17.2), (15-12-1793).
20 Victoria STC, 814, (17.1), (27-11-1792).
21 H.R.O. - 2M69. (Item 3)
22 The British Factory in Lisbon. A R Walford. 1940, 73.
23 H.R.O. - 2M69. (Item 1)
24 The Benevolent Burns of Richmond Hill, Richard J Smith. (Richmond Local Studies).
25 H.R.O. - 2M69. (Item 1) (7-05-1793)
26 H.R.O. - 2M69. (Item 3) (12-08-1793)
27 H.R.O. - M449.
28 H.R.O. - 2M69. (Item 3) (12-08-1793)
29 H.R.O. - 2M69. (Item 3) (12-08-1793)
30 Victoria STC, 816, (17.3), (22-11-1794).
31 Tom Poole and his Friends - 1888 - Mrs H Sandford, 1, 96.
32 The Early Life of Robert Southey 1774-1803 - William Haller - 1917, 168
33 H.R.O. - 2M69. (Item 5) (26-10-1794)
34 Victoria STC, 817, (17.4), (22-09-1795.).
35 The Common Place Book of John May.
36 Victoria STC. 814 - 934.
37 Warter, Vol 1, 33, (4-06-1797).
38 Warter, Vol 1,44, (10-09-1797).
39 Ramos, 3.
40 The Early Life of Robert Southey 1774-1803 - William Haller - 1917, 214.
41 Warter, Vol 1, 53, (6-04-1798).
42 University of Leeds, Special Collections, Brotherton Library.
43 Ramos, 30. (5-05-1798). Warter, Vol 4, 502, (5-04-1837).
44 Ramos, 39. (11-11-1798).
45 Victoria STC. 814 - 934.
46 Victoria STC, 827, (17.14), (3-02-1799).
47 Victoria STC, 829, (17.16), (31-07-1799).
48 Warter, Vol 1, 78, (29-07-1799).
49 Warter, Vol 1, 81, (3-09-1799).
50 Warter, Vol 1, 101, (2-04-1800).
51 Ramos, 58. (1-09-1800).
52 Ramos, 55. (12-04-1800).
53 University of Leeds, Special Collections, Brotherton Library.
54 H.R.O. - 2M69. (Item 17) (12-12-1799)
55 Victoria STC, 831, (17.18), (10-01-1800).
56 Victoria STC, 832, (17.19), (15-02-1800).
57 Ramos, 58. (2-05-1800).
58 Ramos, 61. (1-09-1800).
59 Warter, Vol 1, 127, (29-10-1800).
60 H.R.O. - 2M69. Copy/687, 27.
61 Victoria STC, 843, (17.30), (3-07-1801).
62 Rev C.C. Southey, 145 (13-04-1801).
63 Ramos, 62. (11-07-1801).
64 Ramos, 63. (16-10-1801).
65 Victoria STC, 844, (17.31), (31-07-1801).
66 H.R.O. - 2M69. Copy/687, 35.1802 - 1822
67 Rev C.C. Southey, 155 (25-07-1802).
68 Warter, Vol 1, 196, (2-06-1802).
69 Warter, Vol 1, 199, (7-06-1802).
70 Ramos, 66. (5-09-1802).
71 Warter, Vol 1, 205, (23-11-1802).
72 Ramos, 71. (7-01-1803).
73 Coleridge Fille - Earl Leslie Griggs - 1940 (Oxford University Press), 48.

74 Victoria STC, 853, (17.40), (13-02-1803).
75 H.R.O. - 2M69. Copy/687, 39.
76 H.R.O. - 2M69. (Items 22-24). (2-1803)
77 Ramos, 73. (23-02-1803).
78 Victoria STC, 856, (17.43), (20-03-1803).
79 Ramos, 73. (19-04-1803).
80 Warter, Vol 1, 215, (Bristol 1803).
81 H.R.O. - 2M69. (Item 26).(19-06-1803)
82 Ramos, 77. (5-05-1803).
83 Warter, Vol 1, 220, (20-07-1803).
84 Warter, Vol 1, 229, (19-08-1803).
85 Ramos, 91. (24-12-1803).
86 Rev C.C. Southey, 161 (9-06-1803).
87 Warter, Vol 1, 234, (22-09-1803).
88 Victoria STC, 858, (17.45), (24-12-1803).
89 Rev. C.C. Southey, 175 (8-03-1804).
90 Ramos, 82. (10-11-1803).
91 H.R.O. - 2M69. Copy/687, 46.
92 H.R.O. - 2M69. (Item 27). (5-02-1805)
93 H.R.O. - 2M69. (Items 28 & 29).
94 Warter, Vol 1, 339, (5-08-1805).
95 H.R.O. - 2M69. Copy/687, 50.
96 Ramos, 104. (24-11-1805).
97 Warter, Vol 1, 391, (18-06-1806).
98 Ramos, 111. (24-10-1806).
99 H.R.O. - 2M69. (Item 36). 917-02-1807).
100 Collected Letters of Samuel Taylor Coleridge Volume III, Edited by Earl Leslie Griggs, 1959. 6 (2-04-1807), 24 (8-1807)
101 Letter from John May to Mrs Moore, sister in law of his brother Joseph, dated 12-11-1830 & explaining past financial arrangements. Transcribed by his sister, Susan Louisa May.
102 H.R.O. - 2M69. 42M66/226 - Abstract of Title - Hale Manor.
103 Warter, Vol 2, 8, 42.
104 Victoria STC, 869, (17.56), (12-12-1806).
105 Warter, Vol 2, (26-10-1807).
106 Warter, Vol 2, (1-12-1807).
107 H.R.O. - 2M69. Copy/687, 67.
108 Warter, Vol 2, 42, (16-12-1807).
109 Warter, Vol 2, 45, (17-12-1807).
110 Warter, Vol 2, 35, (19-12-1807), 36, (21-12-1807).
111 H.R.O. - 2M69. Copy/687, 72.
112 Ramos, 115. (16-04-1808).
113 Warter, Vol 2, 80, (29-06-1808).
114 H.R.O. - 2M69. Copy/687, 73.
115 Victoria STC, 941, (17.125), (13-09-1808).
116 H.R.O. - 2M69. (Item 39).
117 Warter, Vol 2, 178, (16-11-1809).
118 Ramos, 121. (9-08-1810).
119 H.R.O. - 2M69. Copy/687, 78.
120 H.R.O. - 2M69. Copy/687, 83.
121 Warter, Vol 3, 256, (15-06-1821).
122 Collected Letters of Samuel Taylor Coleridge Volume III, Edited by Earl Leslie Griggs,1959.296, 297. (11-1810).
123 H.R.O. - 2M69. Copy/687, 85, 87.

124 Victoria STC, 872, (17.59), (21-01-1811).
125 Victoria STC, 874, (17.61), (28-02-1811).
127 Victoria STC, 874, (17.61), (28-02-1811).
128 Victoria STC, 878, (17.65), (20-05-1811).
129 Victoria STC, 877, (17.64), (10-04-1811).
130 Bodleian Library Oxford. MS. Eng. Lett. c.289, fol 2. (1-04-1811).
131 Victoria STC, 877, (17.64), (10-04-1811).
132 Bodleian Library Oxford. MS. Eng. Lett. c.289, fol 4.
133 Lord Coleridge - 1905, 190.
134 Specimens of the Table Talk of the late Samuel Taylor Coleridge .[Edited by H. N. Coleridge] 1884, 274.
135 Unpublished letters of Samuel Taylor Coleridge, Earl L. Griggs, 1932, 136. (27-09-1815).
136 Collected Letters of Samuel Taylor Coleridge Volume III, Edited by Earl Leslie Griggs, 1959. 400 (4-05-1812).
137 Victoria STC, 942, (17.126), (24-08-1811).
138 Victoria STC, 880, (17.67), (6-10-1811).
139 Victoria STC, 881, (17.68), (22-12-1811).
140 Warter, Vol 2, 245, (24-11-1811).
141 Bodleian Library Oxford. MS. Eng. Lett. c.289, fol 8. (8-12-1811).
142 Victoria STC, 881, (17.68), (22-12-1811).
143 Victoria STC, 881, (17.68), (22-12-1811).
144 Bodleian Library Oxford. MS. Eng. Lett. c.289, fol 16. (3-02-1812).
145 Greenwich Heritage Centre.
146 Bodleian Library Oxford. MS. Eng. Lett. c.289, fol 14. (26-10-1812).
147 Rev C.C. Southey, 278 (2-11-1811).
148 Victoria STC, 891, (17.78), (16-09-1813).
149 The Life of the Rev Andrew Bell - Robert Southey - 1844.
150 Victoria STC, 884, (17.71), (10-08-1812).
151 Ramos, 125. (28-08-1812).
152 Rev C.C. Southey, 286 (14-08-1812).
153 H.R.O. - 2M69. Copy/687, 104.
154 Bodleian Library Oxford. MS. Eng. Lett. c.289, fol 27. (20-11-1812).
155 Victoria STC, 888, (17.75), (28-01-1813).
156 Victoria STC, 888, (17.75), (28-01-1813).
157 Ramos, 128. (29-08-1813).
158 H.R.O. - 2M69. (Item 65). (15-05-1816).
159 Ramos, 128. (29-08-1813).
160 Ramos, 140. (15-01-1815).
161 Victoria STC, 893, (17.80), (16-01-1813).
162 Lord Coleridge - 1905, 12.
163 University of Leeds, Special Collections, Brotherton Library, (28-11-1813).
164 Lord Coleridge - 1905, 210, (24-03-1814)
165 Bodleian Library Oxford. MS. Eng. Lett. c.289, fol 48. (29-06-1814).
166 Lord Coleridge - 1905, 208, (24-01-1814).
167 Warter, Vol 2, 356, (1-07-1814).
168 H.R.O. - 2M69. (Item 59). (23-11-1814).
169 Victoria STC, 900, (17.87), (29-11-1814).

173

170 Birmingham Reference Library, Barnard Collection, MS3192/Acc 1941 - 03/558 dated 1814.
171 Victoria STC, 896, (17.83), 936, (17.123), 898, (17.85).
172 Ramos, 130. (18-02-1814).
173 The Collected Works of S.T Coleridge. Edited by J.C.C. Mays - 2001.
174 Ramos, 134. (15-07-1814).
175 Ramos, 136. (10-09-1814).
176 Lord Coleridge - 1905, 214.
177 Victoria STC, 899, (17.86), (23-09-1814).
178 Ramos, 140. (15-01-1815). 142. (20-03-1815).
179 Ramos, 171. (28-12-1818).
180 Ramos, 175. (22-05-1819).
181 Victoria STC, 901, (17.88), (25-03-1815).
182 The Poet's Pilgimage to Waterloo by Robert Southey, Poet Laureate. Longman etc. 1816.
183 Provost and Fellows of Eton College - Archives - ED/9 & Dr Keate's Register.
184 Lord Coleridge - 1905, 268.
185 Victoria STC, 902, (17.89), (22-09-1815).
186 Rev C.C. Southey, 345 (1-01-1817).
187 Warter, Vol 3, 46, (18-10-1816).
188 Bodleian Library Oxford. MS. Eng. Lett. c.290, fol 18. (02-1817).
189 Ramos, 155. (11-05-1817).
190 Victoria STC, 913, (17.100), (8-10-1817).
191 Victoria STC, 915, (17.102), (30-06-1818).
192 A History of Eton College 1440 - 1910. Sir Maxwell Lyte KCB. Macmillan. 1911, 376.
193 Provost and Fellows of Eton College - Archives - ED/9.
194 Provost and Fellows of Eton College, Archives, Diary of Miss Margareta Brown, Vol XXV.
195 Provost and Fellows of Eton College - Archives - ED/9/3.
196 Provost and Fellows of Eton College - Archives - ED/9/1.
197 Provost and Fellows of Eton College, Archives, Diary of Miss Margareta Brown, Vol XXV.
198 Provost and Fellows of Eton College - Archives - ED/9/6
199 Eton of Old or Eighty Years Since. 1811 - 1822, by An Old Colleger, 1892.
200 Victoria STC, 917, (17.104), (8-11-1818).
201 Victoria STC, 918, (17.105), (9-11-1818).
202 Victoria STC, 949, (17.133), (10-11-1818).
203 Bodleian Library Oxford. MS. Eng. Lett. c.290, fol 38. (13-11-1818).
204 Rev C.C. Southey, 367 (16-11-1818).
205 Victoria STC, 950, (17.134), (6-12-1818).
206 Bodleian Library Oxford. MS. Eng. Lett. c.290, fol 39. (22-12-1818).
207 Ramos, 170. (28-12-1818).
208 H.R.O. - 2M69. (Item 68). (11-02-1819).
209 Bodleian Library Oxford. MS. Eng. Lett. c.290, fol 41. (02-1819).
210 Bodleian Library Oxford. MS. Eng. Lett. c.289, fol 64. (10-02-1819).
211 Bodleian Library Oxford. MS. Eng. Lett. c.290, fol 43. (31-03-1819).
212 Victoria STC, 951, (17.135), (4-04-1819).
213 Bodleian Library Oxford. MS. Eng. Lett. c.290, fol 1. (25-11-1819).
214 Victoria STC, 918, (17.105), (9-11-1819).
215 Ramos, 180. (13-09-1819).
216 Ramos, 173. (14-03-1819).
217 Bodleian Library Oxford. MS. Eng. Lett. c.289, fol 61. (19-11-1819).
218 Life of Thomas Arnold, D.D. Head-Master of Rugby, A. P. Stanley, - 1904, 33.
219 Victoria STC, 920, (17.107), (19-01-1820).
220 Victoria STC, 924, (17.111), (10-12-1820).
221 Ramos, 193. (10-04-1822).
222 Samuel Taylor Coleridge Collection, Victoria University Library (Toronto). 21 ff. (SMS F1.3) & The Collected Works of Samuel Taylor Coleridge, Poetical Works I Poems (Variorum text): Part I Edited by J.C.C. Mays. Bollingen Series LXXV Princeton University Press. 166. B.2. (& p 10, 12, 18, 19, 20, 23, 31, 43, 64, 66, 67, 166).
223 The Notebooks of Samuel Taylor Coleridge Edited by Kathleen Coburn. Volume 3 1808 - 1819. Notes. [4055], [4073]. Routledge & Kegan Paul - 1973.
224 The Collected Works of Samuel Taylor Coleridge, Poetical Works I Poems (Reading Text):Part 2 Edited by J.C.C. Mays. Bollingen Series LXXV Princeton University Press. Annexe A, 1164.
225 University of Leeds - Special Collections - Brotherton Library.
226 H.R.O. - 2M69.
227 Victoria STC, 920, (17.107), (19-01-1820).
228 Bodleian Library Oxford. MS. Eng. Lett. c.289, fol 83. (7-04-1820).
229 Victoria STC, 952, (17.136), (12-04-1820).
230 Victoria STC, 952, (17.136), (12-04-1820).
231 Victoria STC, 922, (17.109), 953, (17.137), 923, (17.110).
232 Victoria STC, 927, (17.114), (21-06-1821).
233 H.R.O. - 42M66/226 - Abstract of Title - Hale Manor.
234 Warter, Vol 3, 254, (15-06-1821).
235 Rev C.C. Southey, 405 .
236 Exeter College, University of Oxford - records.
237 Victoria STC, 929, (17.116), (22-02-1822).
238 Victoria STC, 929, (17.116), (22-02-1822).
239 Keswick Museum and Art Gallery, Southey letters, 122, (19-03-1822).
240 Bodleian Library Oxford. MS. Eng. Lett. c.289, fol 107. (31-03-1822).
241 Ramos, 192. (3-03-1822).
242 Ramos, 194. (22-04-1822).
243 Keswick Museum and Art Gallery, Southey letters, 217, (8-05-1822).

244 Keswick Museum and Art Gallery, Southey letters, 125, (22-07-1822).
245 Ramos, 195. (25-07-1822).
246 Warter, Vol 3, 322, (30-07-1822).
247 A Guide to All the Watering and Sea Bathing Places, J Feltham - 1825, 353.
248 Soho Foundry - W.K.V. Gale - W & T Avery Ltd, 1946.
249 Collected Letters of Samuel Taylor Coleridge Volume III, Edited by Earl Leslie Griggs, 1959. 371, (18-12-1812).
250 Eton School Lists 1791-1877 - H.E.C. Stapylton - Eton: R.Ingalton Drake - 1885.
251 Warter, Vol 3, 324, (17-08-1822).
252 Rev C.C. Southey, 410 (16-09-1822).
253 Keswick Museum and Art Gallery, Southey letters, 221, (31-08-1822).
254 Warter, Vol 3, 328, (9-09-1822).
255 The Life of the Rev Andrew Bell, Robert Southey, 1844, Vol 3, 556.
256 The Life of the Rev Andrew Bell, Robert Southey, 1844, Vol 3, 423 et seq
257 Ramos, 195. (13-09-1822).
258 Victoria STC, 930, (17.117), (5-09-1822).
259 Bodleian Library Oxford. MS. Eng. Lett. c.289, fol 112. (22-10-1822).
260 Ramos, 197. (5-12-1822).
261 Coleridge Fille - Earl Leslie Griggs - 1940, 48 et seq.
262 Lord Coleridge - 1905, 282, (22-03-1823).
263 Minnow among Tritons. Mrs S.T.Coleridge's Letters to Thomas Poole, 1799-1834, (1934) 99.
264 Ramos, 204. (2-08-1823).
265 The Wordsworth Trust, Dove Cottage, Grasmere, Cumbria WLMS A / Coleridge, Sara / 7. 21-09-1823).
266 Minnow among Tritons. Mrs S.T.Coleridge's Letters to Thomas Poole, 1799-1834 (1934) 10.
267 Coleridge Fille - Earl Leslie Griggs - 1940, 48 (note 2).
268 Coleridge Fille - Earl Leslie Griggs - 1940, 48.
269 The Letters of William and Dorothy Wordsworth E De Selincourt - 1978.
270 Victoria STC, 931, (17.118), (5-08-1823).
271 Warter, Vol 3, 431, (4-07-1824).
272 Ramos, 212. (11-09-1825).
273 H.R.O. - 2M69. (Item 69). (20-10-1825).
274 Exeter College, University of Oxford - records.
275 H.R.O. - 2M69. (Item 70). (6-12-1825).
276 University of Leeds, Special Collections, Brotherton Library.
277 H.R.O. - 2M69. (Item 71). (2-06-1826).
278 Norfolk Record Office, DN/ORD 24 [1826]
279 H.R.O. - 2M69. (Item 72). (6-06-1826).
280 Ramos, 215. (7-01-1826).
281 Ramos, 217. (6-05-1826).
282 Warter, Vol 4, 13, (30-07-1826).
283 Victoria STC, 934, (17.121), (20-08-1826).
284 Ramos, 217. (6-05-1826).
285 Lord Coleridge - 1905, 190.
286 Bodleian Library Oxford. MS. Eng. Lett. c.289, fol 135. (30-09-1826).
287 Ramos, 223. (14-05-1827).
288 The Bank of England From Within - Vol II - W. Marston Acres - (1931) (Oxford University Press), 566-567.
289 A History of Banking in Bristol 1750 - 1899, Charles Henry Cave - Privately Printed - 1899.
290 Warter, Vol 4, 59, (15-09-1827).
291 Rev C.C. Southey, 456 (15-09-1827).
292 Victoria STC, 956, (17.140), (20-01-1828).
293 Bodleian Library Oxford. MS. Eng. Lett. c.289, fol 138. (17-07-1827).
294 Bodleian Library Oxford. MS. Eng. Lett. c.289, fol 142. (5-04-1828).
295 H.R.O. - 2M69. (Item 73). (9-07-1828).
296 Bodleian Library Oxford. MS. Eng. Lett. c.290, fol 104. (9-04-1828).
297 H.R.O. - 2M69. (Item 74). (15-08-1828).
298 Bodleian Library Oxford. MS. Eng. Lett. c.289, fol 144. (1-09-1828).
299 H.R.O. - 2M69. (Item 76). (4-11-1828).
300 H.R.O. - 2M69. (Item 77). (17-11-1828).
301 Bodleian Library Oxford. MS. Eng. Lett. c.289, fol 148. (31-07-1829).
302 Ramos, 234. (11-12-1828).
303 Bodleian Library Oxford. MS. Eng. Lett. c.289, fol 150. (3-11-1829).
304 Ramos, 235. (19-03-1829).
305 Victoria STC, 956, (17.140), (20-01-1828).
306 Victoria STC, 965, (17.145), (7-04-1830).
307 Ramos, 278. (7-11-1835).
308 The Flowers of May - Collins & Brown - 1990, 8.
309 Bodleian Library Oxford. MS. Eng. Lett. c.289, fol 159. (5-06-1830).
310 Bodleian Library Oxford. MS. Eng. Lett. c.289, fol 166. (21-02-1831).
311 Bodleian Library Oxford. MS. Eng. Lett. c.289, fol 185. (2-06-1831).
312 Bodleian Library Oxford. MS. Eng. Lett. c.289, fol 194. (26-09-1831).
313 Ramos, 242. (21-01-1831).
314 Bodleian Library Oxford. MS. Eng. Lett. c.289, fol 176. (14-03-1831), fol 181, (30-05-1831).
315 Ramos, 244. (25-06-1831).
316 Bodleian Library Oxford. MS. Eng. Lett. c.289, fol. 185. (23-06-1831), fol 190, (24-07-1831).
317 Rev C.C. Southey, 506 (27-12-1831).
318 The Bank of England From Within - Vol II - W. Marston Acres - (1931) (Oxford University Press), 566-567.
319 Ramos, 250. (30-11-1831).
320 Ramos, 247. (1-10-1831).
321 A History of Banking in Bristol 1750 - 1899, Charles Henry Cave - Privately Printed - 1899.
322 Lord Coleridge - 1905, 307.
323 Bodleian Library Oxford. MS. Eng. Lett. c.289, fol 164. (23-12-1830).

324 Bodleian Library Oxford. MS. Eng. Lett. c.289, fol 168. (27- Birmingham 02-1831).
325 Bodleian Library Oxford. MS. Eng. Lett. c.289, fol 194. (26-09-1831).
326 Bodleian Library Oxford. MS. Eng. Lett. c.290, fol 22. (1-05-1833).
327 H.R.O. - 2M69.42M66/226 - Abstract of Title - Hale Manor.
328 Birmingham Reference Library, Barnard Collection, MS 3192/Acc1941-301 1843.
329 Rev C.C. Southey, 514 (1-03-1833).
330 Letters from a Hackney Curate, Richard J Smith, Hackney History Volume 2 - 1996, 22.
331 The University of York, Institution Act Book 20.
332 East Riding of Yorkshire Record Office.
333 The University of York, Clerical Guide 1836.
334 The National Gazetteer of Great Britain and Ireland (1868) & Bulmer's History and Directory of East Yorkshire (1892).
335 Ramos, 264. (2-05-1834).
336 H.R.O. - 2M69.42M66/226 - Abstract of Title - Hale Manor.
337 Ramos, 265. (2-05-1834).
338 Rev C.C. Southey, 522 (2-05-1834).
339 Ramos, 266. (29-08-1834).
340 Rev C.C. Southey, 530 (30-03-1835).
341 Ramos, 272. (6-05-1835).
342 Ramos, 275. (1-08-1835).
343 Ramos, 276. (7-11-1835).
344 Greenwich Heritage Centre.
345 Warter, Vol 4, 528, (27-08-1837)
346 Warter, Vol 4, 569, (4-05-1839)
347 Warter, Vol 4, 572, (7-06-1839), (6-07-1839).
348 H.R.O. - 2M69.
349 Rev C.C. Southey, 563.
350 Birmingham Reference Library, Barnard Collection, MS 3192/Acc1941-301 1843.
351 H.R.O. - 2M69. (Item 126). (5-01-1843).
352 H.R.O. - 2M69. (Item 109). (5-08-1845).
353 A Short History of Ugborough Church, Devonshire, PMB Lake, 1941.
354 A Short History of Ugborough Church, Devonshire, PMB Lake, 1941.
355 Bodleian Library Oxford. MS. Eng. Lett. d.295, Various unbound folios.
356 H.R.O. - 2M69. (Item 78). (29-10-1850).
357 H.R.O. - 2M69. (Item 84). (24-02-1852).
358 Bodleian Library Oxford. MS. Eng. Lett. c.290, fol 159. (23-08-1857).
359 Bodleian Library Oxford. MS. Eng. Lett. c.290, fol 161. (28-04-1857).
360 College of Arms MS Grants 82.87.
361 Birmingham Reference Library, MS 3192/Acc1941-031/574,1864. Kennion Family: Charlotte Livius May.

Further References

Samuel Taylor Coleridge - A Biographical Study - E. K. Chambers - 1938.
Southey - Jack Simmons - 1945.
The May family of Richmond and the Lisbon Factory - Richard Smith. (Richmond Local Studies).
History of Hale Manor - G.L.J. Goff - Edited by Rosalind Pasmore - 1999
Various Wills from National Archives.
Public Census Returns.
Berkshire Record Office
Devon Record Office
East Riding of Yorkshire Record Office.
Birmingham Record Office
Richmond Record Office
British Factory Chaplaincy in Lisbon. Baptism Records 1721 - 1807.
Short Notes on the Church and Parish of Ottery St Mary. Rev Sidney W Cornish. D. D.
Leigh's New Pocket Road book of England, Wales and part of Scotland - 1826.
The King's School A History - G.E.J. Holmes - 1963 Privately Published.
Reminiscences of Samuel Taylor Coleridge and Robert Southey by Joseph Cottle
In Pursuit of Coleridge - Kathleen Coburn - The Bodley Head Ltd - 1977
My Native Home, Samuel Taylor Coleridge of Ottery St Mary, Devon - John Witham - 1984.
Coleridge Darker Reflections - Richard Holmes - Harper Collins - 1998
Eton Established - Tim Card - John Murray, Albemarle Street - 2001
The Notebooks of Samuel Taylor Coleridge Edited by Kathleen Coburn. Volume 3 1808 - 1819. [4073]. Routledge & Kegan Paul - 1973
The Bondage of Love - A Life of Mrs Samuel Taylor Coleridge - Molly Lefebure - Norton & Company - 1986
Boyles Court Guide 1826
Private papers in America.
A History of the Parish of Hale and Woodgreen, Hampshire - Margaret Booth-Jones - 1953 .

Index

Alfoxden 20, 27
Ambleside 80, 85, 163 – 165
Archer, Thomas 14, 120
Arnold Dr 6, 7, 73 - 77, 80, 84, 87
Auction (John May's Library) 120
Awdry, John 42
Bamford Mr (Grasmere Teacher) 85
Bank of England Bristol 6, 95 - 96, 99 109 – 110
Bankrupt 57, 92, 95, 110 – 111
Baring F 27
Barker Miss 28, 36-37
Bassenthwaite 27, 85, 168
Bath 23, 71
Beaumont Lady 91
Bedford, Grosvenor 28, 64, 72
Bedford Square 6, 14, 26, 39, 58
Bell Dr 5 - 6, 47, 67, 84-86, 169
Belle – Savage 132
Birmingham 82-84, 110, 132, 134, 136, 141, 148
Blackburn 155-157
Blackheath 6, 113-115, 117, 118, 120-121
Blackmore, John 80
Bolton 155, 161
Boulton, Mathew 82 - 83, 136-137, 139
Bowles, Caroline 6, 57, 95, 114
Brakspear, Annette 120
Bramshaw 6, 35, 50
Brandling, Charles 50
Brazil 5, 14, 32, 37-39, 47-48, 50, 52-53, 55, 77-79, 92, 95
Bridgewater Arms 82, 154-155
Bristol 6, 15, 19-20, 22-23, 29-30, 32, 54, 95-96, 102, 107, 109-110
Bristol Reform Bill Riots 109
British Factory 6, 8-14, 16-17, 20
Brown, Margaretta Miss 58, 60
Buckmaster Mr 39
Bullion 47
Bures St Mary 94, 96-99
Burns Family 16-17
Burney Charles 46
Cardwell H S 156
Carlisle, Anthony 40
Chester 141, 148-152
Cintra 14, 26, 28
Clarkson, Catherine 88, 91
Clifton 6, 95-97, 107, 111, 113
Coal 141, 143, 148
Coleridge, Edward 22, 23, 53, 65, 71, 77, 89, 91
Coleridge, Frances Duke 45

Coleridge, Francis George 65
Coleridge, George (Rev) 6-7, 15, 18-20, 22-32, 35-36, 38, 41-43, 45-50, 52-56, 58, 62-63, 72, 74-75, 77-79, 86-87, 92, 95-96, 107
Coleridge, George May 15, 58, 115
Coleridge, Hartley 54-55, 75-76, 80, 85, 91
Coleridge, Henry Nelson 43-44, 89, 91, 106
Coleridge, James Duke 64-66, 70-71, 76
Coleridge, James (The Colonel) 15, 36, 38, 42, 51, 54-55, 63, 65, 67, 69-70, 89, 91, 106, 110, 113
Coleridge, John Duke 77
Coleridge, John Taylor 6, 15, 43, 46, 48, 52, 56, 62-63, 70, 73-77, 79-80, 84, 87, 89, 91, 94-97, 99-100, 102-103, 105-106, 108-111, 113
Coleridge Lord 95
Coleridge, Luke Mrs 43
Coleridge Mrs Sara (nee Fricker) 5, 20, 25, 29, 31, 43, 86, 88-89, 91, 113, 169
Coleridge, Samuel Taylor 2, 6-7, 15, 19-20, 23-27, 29, 34-35, 40, 43-44, 53-55, 74-76, 84, 86, 89, 113
Coleridge, Sara 5-7, 29, 75, 86, 88-91, 106-107, 169
Commissioners and Comptrollers 92, 113
Coppendale, John 9, 10, 13
Coppendale, Mary 8, 12
Coppendale, May & Co 10, 12-13
Coppendale, May & Worthington 38
Coppendale, Rose 13
Coppendale, Thomas 13, 16-17, 22, 25, 36, 38, 48, 53, 111
Corry Mr 28
Cottle, Joseph 20-21, 53-54, 96, 113
Cottle, Sarah 113, 119
County Receivership 92
Critical Review 25
Crump, Elizabeth 91
Dea Family 10
Dea, John 114
Dea, Rose 25
Dea, Thomas 13, 111, 114
Derwent Water 27, 92, 168
Dove Cottage 2, 21, 25
Durant, George 143
Duval Mr 26
Earley (Near Reading) 120-122
Earthquake (Lisbon) 11-12
Equitable Insurance Co 15, 58, 121
Eton 2, 5-7, 50, 52, 55-59, 61-62, 64-66, 68, 70, 84, 88, 92, 158
Eton Rebellion 6, 58, 61
Exeter College (Oxford) 7, 75, 79-80, 88-89

177

Exeter Flying Post	115	Lisbon	8-13, 16-18, 20, 23, 25-26, 28, 31, 36-38, 111, 120
Express Packet	50		
Fee Farm Rents	36	Liverpool	36, 85-86, 95, 153, 157
Fixsen, John Frederick (Rev)	120-121	Liverpool Branch Bank	95
Fleming Lady	85	Livius (family)	10, 25
Floating Island	92	Livius, Charlotte	27
Forbes family	18-19, 31, 33-34	Livius, Peter Lewis	25
French wars	6, 14, 32, 36	Livius, Susanna Frances	25
Fricker, Edith	19	Lodge Mr	12
Fricker Mrs	19	Longworth	80
Fricker, Sara	20	Lord Chancellor	99, 103, 111
Gardiner, William	14	**Madoc**	33
Gas – works	134	Madras (system of education)	47, 84-85
Gilpin, William	114	Manchester	80, 82, 84-85, 153-155
Goff, Joseph	113	Marriott	59, 61
Grasmere	2, 21, 23, 25, 32, 40, 47, 80-81, 85, 165-166	Marsh Gate	30-31, 33, 39
		Massien Mr	9
Grasmere school	85	May, Alice Kitson	5, 116, 120-121
Green Ottery Copy Book	6, 74-76	May, Arthur De Kewer Livins	122
Greenwich	2, 46, 115	May, Charlotte Livius	45, 117-119, 121
Greta Hall	25, 27-29, 31, 40, 43, 47, 78, 80, 84, 86, 91, 107, 168-169	May, John Coleridge	114, 116, 121
		May, John Cyril	121-122
Grocer's Company	116	May, John Maunsell Frampton	122
Gun manufactory	139	May, Joseph (John's father)	4, 8-10, 12-14, 17-18, 20, 22
Hackney	5, 7, 15, 75-76, 87, 93, 97-99, 101, 103, 108, 111, 112	May, Joseph (John's brother)	6, 13, 15, 16-17, 25-26, 30-36, 38, 50, 52, 77, 108
Hale	2, 6, 13-17, 19-20, 22, 25-26, 28, 30, 33-38, 40-41, 43, 45, 48, 50, 78, 88, 104, 107-108, 111-112, 119,	May, Joseph (Wicked Joseph)	108, 112
		May, Margaret	9, 13-14, 19, 26-27, 38-39, 58
Hammersmith	43	May, (Aunt) Margaret's Diary	7, 9, 26, 28-29, 33-34, 36, 41
Hanbury, Barnard (Rev)	94		
Heath's Court Ottery	49, 67, 72	May, Margaret Noel	121
Hellvellin	167	May, Margaret (nee Stert)	9, 13, 14
Highgate	88-89, 113	May, Maria Jennings (nee Frampton)	111-114, 117, 120-121
Hill, Herbert (Rev)	81, 84		
Holmpton	112-114	May, Maria Charlotte	113, 117
Hull John	84, 154	May, Mary (nee Coppendale)	8, 9, 12, 14, 35, 36, 50, 52, 92
Isle of Wight	33, 38		
Joan of Arc	22-23	May, Mary Charlotte	32, 117-119
Johnson W (Rev)	85	May, Richard	29
Keate Dr John	57-62	May, Susanna Frances Livius	25-27, 29-30, 32-34, 38-39, 41, 45, 107-108, 111
Keble John	93-94		
Kendal	47, 82, 85, 161-163, 165	May, Susanna Frances	116, 120-121
Keswick	2, 25, 28, 31-32, 43, 47, 82, 84-86, 89, 91, 109, 113-114, 127, 153, 165, 168-169	May, Susanna Louisa	33, 114, 117-119, 121
		May, Thomas	8-14
		May, Thomas Charles	16
Kings School (Ottery)	6, 7, 18, 22, 25, 35, 38, 41, 58	May, William	15, 22, 32, 35-36, 38-39, 47-48, 50, 52, 55, 77, 79, 86, 95, 106, 109-111, 115
Laleham	6-7, 73, 75, 80, 84, 88, 92		
Lancaster	154-155, 157-161	Menet Mr	26
Land Tax	35	Mint	83, 136
		Montagu, Basil	40

178

Mouchet, Felix	9-10	Southey, Edith (nee Fricker)	5, 19-20, 24, 27-29, 31, 43, 57, 113-114, 168
Mylne, Robert	39		
Nail manufactory	139	Southey, Edith May	5, 32, 34, 112, 113-114, 168
Napoleon Bonaparte	14, 32, 36, 38	Southey, Margaret Edith	29-31
Nether Stowey	20	Southey, Robert	1, 5- 7, 13, 15, 19-20, 22-34, 36, 38-40, 43-48, 50--55, 57-58, 64, 66, 72, 76-78, 81-82, 84-86, 88-89, 92, 95-96, 102, 106-107, 109-114, 119-120, 168
Newberry, Samuel	117-119		
Newcome's Academy	15-16, 18		
Norris (Rev)	97-98, 100-106, 108, 112		
Northoram	13, 111	Spry John (Rev)	115-116
Old Friars	14, 24, 26, 28, 30-31	St Aubyn Lady	39
Opium	40, 53-54	St German's Terrace Blackheath	114-115,118-119, 121
Ottery St Mary	6, 7, 15, 18, 22-23, 25, 27, 35-36, 38, 41-42, 45, 47, 51, 58, 62, 65, 68, 70, 72-73, 75-76, 78, 80, 89, 91-92	St Mary Magdalene Church	26, 28
		St Mary's Church Hale	13, 104, 107
		St Thomas's Hospital	100, 102-103, 105
		Stert and May Wine Merchants	53, 77-78
Ottery Fair	42	Stert Family	10, 17, 49
Oxen	146	Stert, Arthur	9, 12, 111
Palk	61	Stert, Fanny	17
Pantisocracy	19-20	Stert, Priscilla	13
Penrith	80, 113	Stert, Richard	13, 17
Pin manufactory	136	Strickland Mr	162
Poet Laureate	51-52	Suffolk	5, 94
Poole, Thomas	19-20, 89, 91	**Tavistock** Street, Bedford Square	6, 14, 26, 39, 58, 94-95, 132
Poor Commission	113		
Portugal	5-6, 8-10, 12-14, 17, 20, 22, 24-26, 28, 32, 36, 38	Tea Caddy Houses, Blackheath	6, 114-115
		Thalaba	25, 30
Preston	157-158	The Wick, Richmond Hill	17, 39-40, 43-44, 50, 52-54, 92, 95, 131
Raekin	143		
Red Lion Grasmere	80	Thirlmere	166-167
Reynolds Sir Joshua	17, 40	Typhus	43
Richmond	1, 5-6, 14-15, 19-20, 22-24, 26-33, 41, 43-45, 47, 50, 52-53, 70, 75, 78, 95, 122, 131	**Ugborough**	9, 115-116, 118, 120-121
		Victoria University Canada	2, 6, 74
Richmond Hill	17, 39,127, 153	**Walpole** Family	17
Rickman, John	28, 32, 36, 84	Warden House Ottery	49
Rigaud Professor	44	Warren, Doctor	38, 45, 50-51
Rio de Janeiro	16, 38, 48, 169	Warter, Edith May (nee Southey)	112, 114
Rydal	47, 73, 82, 84-85, 165, 169	Warter Rev J,W.	109, 112, 114
Rydal Mount	84	Warwick	134-135, 139
Saddleback	167-168	Waterloo	14, 55-56, 154, 160
Scarlet Fever	43	Watt, James	83
Sherman, Mary	120	Weymouth	30
Shooters Hill	121	Wheeler Mr	139, 141
Shrewsbury	143-145	Whip manufactory	140
Simcoe, General	23, 38	Whitaker, Edward	119
Sizergh	162-163	Wolverhampton	141
Skiddaw	27, 168	Wordsworth, Dorothy	20, 25, 91
Slate quarries	165	Wordsworth, William	6, 25, 40, 44, 85
Smallpiece Thomas	121	Wordsworth Trust	2, 21, 23
Soho (Manufactory)	82-83, 136-137	Worthington, John	16, 18, 25, 38
Southey, Cuthbert Charles (Rev)	7, 64, 72, 78, 114		

179

Books Published by Bookcase

Books can be ordered directly from Bookcase, 19 Castle Street, Carlisle, CA3 8SY, 01228 544560, www.bookscumbria.com. Please add £2 for postage.

Keswick Characters: Volume One   £7.99
The first volume of a series by members of the Keswick Museum telling the life stories of the many eminent and interesting people who have llived in Keswick over the years. This volume includes Sir John Bankes, Jonathan Otley, Joseph Richardson & Sons, Henry Cowper Marshall, John Richardson, George Smith - the Skiddaw Hermit, James Clifton Ward, Hardwicke Drummond Rawnsley, Tom Wilson and Ray McHaffie.

The Loving Eye and Skilful Hand: The Keswick School of Industrial Arts.   Ian Bruce.   £15.00
This is the first detailed study of the Keswick School. Founded by the Rawnsleys, the school became one of the most important centres of the Arts and Crafts movement. The book should be of great interest to historians and collectors.

Keswick: The Story of a Lake District Town.   George Bott.   £15
This elegant history tells the story of Keswick from the time of Castlerigg Stone Circle to the present day. Keswick has an importance far beyond its size. German miners came in Elizabethan times, the pencil was discovered here, it was a key centre of the Romantic revolution and later the town became famous for the Keswick Convention.

The Story of the Newlands Valley.   Susan Grant.   £10
Susan Grant's family has lived in the Newlands Valley near Keswick for over 350 years. Her detailed history draws on old records and extensive personal knowledge to paint a picture of a unique isolated community.